Understanding Contemporary American Conservat**ism**

D1523307

Contemporary American conservatism – a mélange of ideas, people, and organizations – is difficult to define; even conservatives themselves are unable to agree about its essential meaning. Yet the conservative movement is well financed, exerts strong influence in the Republican Party, inspires followers throughout the land, and has spawned a network of think tanks and media outlets that are the envy of its competitors. It is a powerful political force with which to be reckoned. This book examines how that has come about and what contemporary conservatism signifies for US politics and policy. It looks at the recent history of conservatism in America as well as its antecedents in the UK, traces changes over time using American National Election Study data from 1972 to the present in what it means when people say they are conservatives, and assesses the prospects for American conservatism, both in the near-term electoral context and over the longer term as well.

Joel D. Aberbach is Distinguished Professor of Political Science and Public Policy, and Director of the Center for American Politics and Public Policy, at the University of California, Los Angeles.

Joel Aberbach has added measurably to his reputation as a highly-regarded political scientist with his brilliant new book on American political conservatism. Focusing on the vigorous and highly ideological Reaganism that has been in force over the last few decades, this illuminating book provides some clues to the sources of this brand of American conservatism. Aberbach also traces American conservatism from the early 20th Century to the mid-century moderate conservatism of President Dwight Eisenhower to the more muscular conservatism of Senator Barry Goldwater, and on to the form of conservatism that was introduced with Ronald Reagan's election in 1981 and modified under George H.W. Bush, George W. Bush, and by Congress members and presidential hopefuls during the Obama years.

James A. Reichley, *Author of* The Life of the Parties: A History of American Political Parties

American conservatism today is a blend of philosophical positions and economic, political, and cultural beliefs and policy preferences that are viewed as conservative because they are promoted by groups that identify as conservative. Its arguments and ideas fuel the perceptions and intentions of Republicans, and distinguish conservatism from current American liberalism. This book methodically elaborates the issue stands of American conservatism and the ever-greater issue cleavages that distinguish it from American progressivism and the politics of Democrats. Almost 70 years ago, American political scientists called for more ideological coherence in the nation's parties. Aberbach does us all a service by identifying the issue divisions that have developed as a consequence of realizing this academic wish.

John R. Petrocik, *University of Missouri*

Understanding Contemporary American Conservatism is a *tour de force* of ideological and behavioral change among the American public, and particularly on the conservative side of the political spectrum, by one of America's foremost political scientists. Aberbach's clear prose and straightforward analytics produce a compelling storyline about the relationship between political ideology, party identification, and voting behavior across four decades. But more than just a focus on changing individual level relationships, Aberbach examines how institutions incentivize or discourage extremist ideological positions. Among other things, he notes the differences in conservatism in Britain and the US, and the varieties of conservatism that exist in the US. This is, simply put, a superb book for documenting and understanding the polarizing politics that has been with us for a while and which seems to be growing stronger.

Bert A. Rockman, *Purdue University*

Understanding Contemporary American Conservatism

Joel D. Aberbach

Routledge
Taylor & Francis Group

NEW YORK AND LONDON

Published 2017
by Routledge
711 Third Avenue, New York, NY 10017

and by Routledge
2 Park Square, Milton Park, Abingdon, Oxon, OX14 4RN

Routledge is an imprint of the Taylor & Francis Group, an informa business

© 2017 Taylor & Francis

Library of Congress Cataloging in Publication Data
Names: Aberbach, Joel D., author.
Title: Understanding contemporary American conservatism / Joel D.
    Aberbach, University of California, Los Angeles.
Description: New York, NY : Routledge, [2017] | Includes index.
Identifiers: LCCN 2016011097| ISBN 9781138679320 (hardback) |
    ISBN 9781138679337 (pbk.) | ISBN 9781315563381 (ebook)
Subjects: LCSH: Conservatism—United States. | United States—Politics and
    government.
Classification: LCC JC573.2.U6 A25 2017 | DDC 320.520973—dc23
LC record available at https://lccn.loc.gov/2016011097

ISBN: 978-1-138-67932-0 (hbk)
ISBN: 978-1-138-67933-7 (pbk)
ISBN: 978-1-315-56338-1 (ebk)

Typeset in Sabon
by Swales & Willis Ltd, Exeter, Devon, UK

Printed and bound in the United States of America by Publishers Graphics,
LLC on sustainably sourced paper.

Contents

Figures

Tables

Preface

It is almost impossible these days to turn on the news and not hear something about conservatism. Candidates for office on the Republican side compete for the conservative mantle, debating who is the truer conservative and what issue position is the more legitimately conservative. Self-proclaimed conservatives in the Congress go so far as to threaten to close down the government unless they get their way, and the threat is not an idle one since they have done so in the past. A lively conservative media, the writings of conservative media figures and intellectuals, and the seemingly endless words of conservative politicians make notions of conservatism available to almost anyone who is willing to read or hear them.

My interest in the subject grows partly from the omnipresence and successes of conservatism in contemporary American politics and partly from a course I have taught with colleagues at UCLA for many years. The course is on America in the 1960s, and each time I teach it I think back to the heady days of the 1960s, and especially the period immediately after the landslide election of 1964, when to many the US seemed poised to enter a period marked not only by significant social change, but by a set of policy changes that completed the New Deal and would result in an era of liberal dominance.

Well, it didn't quite work out that way, and this book examines one aspect of why this is so; the emergence of a politically powerful conservatism that has penetrated deeply into popular politics in the United States. There are many ways one could look into this phenomenon. My own background led me to focus on analysis of some of the plentiful survey data available on the subject, but there are obviously many other ways one could go. The book contains some intellectual and political history, some comparisons of the views of various governmental elites with those of the general public, and some comparisons of the United States and the United Kingdom with respect to the ways in which their conservative parties have reacted to situations where they have not had electoral success, but the emphasis is on the attitudes and opinions of the US public and the transformation that has taken place in the structure of those attitudes and opinions over the major period covered by the survey data used in the book, 1972–2012.

The basic theme is that conservatism was the modal position of the US public by 1972, probably in reaction to the turmoil that the country experienced in the latter part of the 1960s and into the 1970s, but that this is only part of the story. An equally important part is a deepening of the meaning of conservatism among the general public through these years, with stronger relationships between expressed conservatism and a set of attitudes and social practices that adds depth of meaning to the term for many people. That, and the greater participation in politics by those who feel the most intensely conservative, has contributed greatly to the influence, indeed the force, of conservatism in contemporary American politics.

So, my first debt is to the students and faculty in the UCLA course on "America in the Sixties." They got me started on what has been an interesting odyssey. I have been fortunate also to be a part of two projects that contributed greatly to my understanding of contemporary American conservatism. The first was the Institutions of American Democracy project, organized by Kathleen Jamieson of the Annenberg School for Communication and the Annenberg Public Policy Center at the University of Pennsylvania, and sponsored by the Annenberg Foundation Trust at Sunnylands. My colleague Mark A. Peterson and I co-chaired the Commission on the Executive Branch as part of the project, and co-edited a research volume on the subject as well as contributing to a broader work, *A Republic Divided* (Oxford University Press, 2007), that confronted many of the contentious issues impacting democratic life in the United States.

The survey work done for the Annenberg project deepened my interest in conservatism and led to collaboration with Gillian Peele of Lady Margaret Hall, University of Oxford, on a conference held at the University of Oxford in 2008. Papers from this conference were published in a co-edited volume entitled *Crisis of Conservatism?: The Republican Party, the Conservative Movement, and American Politics after Bush* (Oxford University Press, 2011). My contribution to the latter volume, based on analysis of the Institutions of American Democracy Project survey data, further heighted my interest in the subject, and I have been working on it since, including in this book where Chapter 6 extends work done for the 2011 volume.

I have many people and organizations to thank. First, thanks to the American National Election Studies (ANES) for data available through the Inter-University Consortium for Political and Social Research (ICPSR). These data are the backbone of the book. Thanks also to the Institutions of American Democracy project for sponsoring collection of the data on political elites and the public which are key to Chapter 6. In both cases, of course, the interpretations are mine and I am responsible xii *Preface*

for any errors. Thanks to Libbie Stephenson and Jamie Jamieson of the UCLA Social Science Data Archive; they helped me numerous times in ways large and small. My appreciation to John Wiley & Sons for permission to include parts of my essay on "Understanding American Political Conservatism" in this book. The full essay can be found in *Emerging Trends in the Social and Behavioral Sciences*, edited by Robert Scott and Stephan Kosslyn (John Wiley & Sons, 2015). Thanks to Nuffield College at the University of Oxford where I was Politics Visitor in the Trinity Term of 2011 and a frequent user of the College's excellent library and participant in enlightening conversations about UK politics, and to the people at Oxford's Rothermere American Institute. Finally, many thanks to the Institute for the Study of the Americas at the University of London where I was a visitor in mid-May of 2012, and to the colleagues, friends and others with whom I have discussed conservatism over the years.

I also want to thank the many students at UCLA who helped with various parts of the research and manuscript preparation; Jennifer Patton, Sarah Hadburg, R. Brian Law, Hovannes Abramyan, Sylvia Yu Friedel, Natalie Dreyer, and Katie Westbrook all helped with computer runs or table and figure preparation, or both. Thomas Flaherty was a huge help in the final stages of the project. My colleague David Sears provided great support, both through his knowledge of the literature and his helpful comments. Thanks also to my brother-in-law, Jerry Gross, and my son, Ian Aberbach, both of whom graciously read and commented on the last chapter in the book. And thanks are certainly due to the UCLA Center for American Politics and Public Policy (CAPPP) and its administrator, Carol Wald, and to Jennifer Knerr of Routledge who is an encouraging and supportive editor.

Last, but certainly not least, my spouse, Joan Aberbach, put up with me as I slowly worked my way through the project. I would not have been so patient.

1 Contemporary American Conservatism as a Legacy of the 1960s

An Introduction

From the vantage point of 2016 American conservatism and what is loosely called the American conservative movement (a mélange of ideas, people and organizations) looks like a behemoth, though an often ungainly and troubled one. While the last president conservatives backed left office in 2009, the conservative movement is well financed, has huge influence in the Republican Party, has followers throughout the land, and has a network of think tanks and media outlets that are the envy of its competitors. But it was not always such. Indeed, in 1964 it appeared American conservatism had failed a major test and might be headed for the dustbin of history. However, following the scorching defeat of Barry Goldwater in the 1964 election there emerged a strong conservative movement and a reinvigorated Republican Party that won seven of the next fourteen presidential elections and in 1994 took over both houses of Congress for the first time in many years, and has continued to control at least one house of Congress for much of the period since. This book examines what made all this possible and what contemporary conservatism means for the United States. It focuses on how prominent identification as a conservative is in the United States, what people who call themselves conservatives believe, and how the structure of conservative beliefs has evolved over time.

Perhaps the most famous line written by the conservative William F. Buckley, Jr. appeared in the inaugural issue of *National Review* (1955). Buckley said of his newly-born magazine: "It stands athwart history yelling Stop."[1] At the time, few but the small circle around Buckley thought that conservatism would achieve its current position in American politics, and probably fewer still thought that it would develop in the ways that it has. Inside of a decade, the conservatives' favorite (Senator Goldwater) won the Republican nomination for President, lost the election in a landslide, and then the conservative movement came roaring back, reaching high points (or low points, if one disagreed with its thrusts) in the administrations of Ronald Reagan and George W. Bush. While conservatism has hardly achieved a smaller state – compare the expenditures of the American government at the start and end of the Reagan administration

(Federal outlays in 1981 were $679.2 billion and they were $1,064.4 billion in 1988) and then at the start and end of the administration of George W. Bush ($1,862.8 billion in 2001 and $2,982.5 billion in 2008)[2] – it has surely reached into the lives of Americans and affected how they live and how their government operates.

Before going to a description and analysis of how and why all this happened, it is useful to step back a bit and ask what conservatism is and how it has evolved in the contemporary United States.

What Is Conservatism?

The plain fact of the matter is that there is no universally accepted definition of conservatism. George Nash, perhaps the leading contemporary intellectual historian of conservatism, makes this point in the introduction to his magisterial volume on *The Conservative Intellectual Movement in America Since 1945*, and he is surely right that the content of conservatism is heavily a function of time and place.[3] Conservatives are trying to conserve something, but what they are trying to conserve may no longer exist or may even be defined in terms of an ideal world. Ordinarily, however, conservatism is marked by resistance to ideas and policies that are advocated by non-conservatives or by skepticism about changes emerging from social or economic developments in the broader society.

Samuel Huntington identifies what he calls three theories of conservatism as an ideology. One is that conservatism is the ideology of the aristocracy, and derives from the resistance of the aristocracy to changes in the latter part of the eighteenth century and the first fifty years or so of the nineteenth century. A second is that conservatism is "defined in terms of universal values such as justice, order, balance, [and] moderation." This is obviously closer to the ideal end of the spectrum than to the pure conserving end. Finally, conservatism may be defined as "the passionate affirmation of the value of existing institutions," an affirmation likely to be most virulent when those institutions appear to be under challenge.

Huntington, in general agreement with most scholars, focuses on Edmund Burke as the "conservative archetype" whose ideas form the basis (or, as Huntington calls them, the "basic elements") of conservatism as we generally think about it today. These include the idea that religion is at the very foundation of civil society, that "existing institutions embody the wisdom of previous generations," that experience is superior by far to theory as a guide to proper behavior, that social classes and hierarchy are natural features of society, and, quoting Burke directly, that one should be biased "in favour of any settled scheme of government against any untried product" since reforms are likely to make things worse rather than better.

Further, as Huntington notes, Burkean conservatism, unlike most ideologies, lacks a "substantive ideal." The institutions that evolve may differ according to time and place, so that what is conservative in one context may be quite the opposite in another. This is an extraordinarily important point because Burkean conservatism is not reactionary – it does not oppose change at all costs. Indeed, it encompasses the acceptance of changes that become institutionalized and there is a kind of cautious dynamism about it.[4]

Chris Patten, then a Tory (Conservative) Member of Parliament (and now the Chancellor of the University of Oxford), wrote a quite revealing book in 1983, laying out *The Tory Case*. Drawing on Ian Gilmour (*Inside Right: A Study of Conservatism*, Hutchinson, 1977), he dates the origin of the modern Conservative Party to Burke and the Portland Whigs joining Pitt the Younger as Britain faced dealing with the aftermath of the French Revolution of 1789. Patten stresses that the characteristics marking conservatism in Britain were established in this period. They include a "belief in evolution rather than revolution, [and] a preference for prudence rather than logic," a "defence of property and order and an organic view of society," and "an unashamed patriotism."[5] Patten goes on to say a bit later: "Seeking to conserve the best of the past, trying neither to preserve everything nor to prevent the arrival of tomorrow, is the hallmark of a Conservative." He then quotes Burke: "A disposition to preserve and an ability to improve, taken together, would be my standard of a statesman."[6]

I shall return to a comparison of British and American conservatism later in the book, but for the moment it is sufficient to point out that Patten sees it as very different from many of the strands in modern American conservatism.[7] It is those strands and the somewhat tumultuous evolution of American conservatism that makes it both fascinating and frustrating, both for those who study it as well as for many of its adherents.

Mainstream American conservatism before World War II and in its immediate aftermath, especially in the Republican Party, shared some important elements with the type of conservatism described in the paragraphs above. The leading conservative figure in the Republican Party was arguably Senator Robert Taft of Ohio. He rose to the top of the party in the Senate and was a major contender several times for the party's nomination for president. His political nickname, "Mr. Republican," says it all about his standing. Taft's failures to win the presidential nomination came from the triumph of those in the party (particularly the "Eastern establishment" that Barry Goldwater and his followers so despised) who felt that the country would not support someone with his views and instead backed Wendell Wilkie, Thomas E. Dewey, and Dwight D. Eisenhower to carry the party's banner.

What did Taft believe? The picture painted by James T. Patterson's biography is one of a man who might not be a lock for the title "Mr. Republican" (or, indeed, "Mr. Conservative") today. He was an isolationist and an opponent of executive dominance of foreign policy, and even in the post-war period voted against the NATO treaty and made clear his view that the US could not solve the world's problems and should be fearful that it could "slop into an attitude of imperialism where war becomes an instrument of public policy rather than its last resort."[8] He was "very bright but . . . impatient with abstractions," a villain to the labor movement because of his sponsorship of the Taft-Hartley Act, but also a supporter of the right to strike; a supporter of some basic social benefit policies such as public housing and federal aid to education (though with the reprehensible blinders about civil rights that unfortunately marked many of the men in his generation) as a practical means to "preservation of the family by ensuring it a decent environment"; and a proponent of a floor under income. His biographer notes that following his death in 1953 "no one remained with force enough to restrain the right wing of the party, and Democrats like Lyndon Johnson in the Senate and Sam Rayburn in the House had to stay the impetuous thrusts of men like Barry Goldwater to make possible even the limited legislative accomplishments of Eisenhower's presidency."[9]

Without taking a stand on who was impetuous, it is clear that conservatives were, as Lee Edwards of the Heritage Foundation describes them, "a disputatious lot."[10] In the 1950s and 1960s they were mainly divided between traditionalists and libertarians, and much ink has spilt in later periods elaborating more complex divisions. However, the early 1960s witnessed both an attempt to meld the disparate intellectual strands into a unified movement ("fusionism") and success in nominating an assertively conservative candidate (Barry Goldwater) who, to use the words of one of his campaign slogans, presented "A choice, not an echo."

Fusionism, whose founding is identified with Frank Meyer of the *National Review*, sought to unify traditional conservatives and libertarians through their intensely shared anti-communism.[11] And Goldwater's success in achieving the 1964 Republican nomination was a triumph of conservative insurgents over the Republican establishment (Eastern and otherwise) that had successfully nominated more moderate candidates. Indeed, Goldwater's candidacy was, in many ways, a celebration of a new-found vigor in practical politics that accompanied a surging interest in the intellectual tenets underlying the various notions about what it means to be a conservative.[12]

Goldwater's book, *The Conscience of a Conservative*, was a snappy and provocative statement presenting conservative ideas in a way that inspired many people (and frightened still more when they heard about the contents). While Goldwater lost the election decisively (getting less than 40 percent of the vote), his campaign left a set of legacies that reverberate today: 1. He took a states' rights stand on civil rights, cementing the African American vote as a Democratic vote and laying a firm foundation for the "Southern strategy" that has marked Republican national campaigns since and remade Southern (and national) politics in the process. 2. He gave conservatives a taste of electoral victory in nominating politics and inspired a generation of activists who eventually rose from the ashes of his defeat. 3. While many Republican office holders distanced themselves from Goldwater's campaign, Ronald Reagan gave what came to be known as "the speech" in support of him, an act that cemented Reagan as a major figure in the conservative world. 4. Ironically, Goldwater's overwhelming defeat in the Democratic landslide of 1964 and the accompanying extraordinary and liberal Democratic majorities in Congress paved the way for the flood of Great Society legislation that passed in 1965, legislation that was (and, in many cases, still is) anathema to many conservatives, thereby energizing the movement. (While the Voting Rights Act of 1965 was particularly important in reshaping Southern politics to the benefit of the conservative wing of the Republican Party, contemporary American politics also still reverberates with lingering debates about Medicare, anti-pollution programs and the like.) 5. Finally, the Vietnam War, heavily identified with Johnson, along with the upheavals in society that we know today simply by the term "the sixties" (actually a period that went roughly from 1965 to 1974), repelled many people, some of whom disagreed with the substance of the changes and others with the style of the change agents. This lack of legitimacy created a climate of distrust in government that has bedeviled the liberal, progressive wing of the political spectrum and been a boon to conservatives. In short, overwhelming defeat ultimately gave birth to a re-energized conservative movement and constituency that eventually re-shaped American politics.

While the turmoil of the sixties was ultimately a boon to conservatism and, along with anti-communism, fostered an important degree of cooperation among those who found both the Great Society and many of the movements of the sixties threatening, it did not lead to intellectual consensus. The academic literature about conservatism, and often the public debates, are replete with references not only to traditionalism (sometimes called paleo-conservatism) and libertarianism, but to neo-conservatism, the religious right (a vigorous political force, especially since the founding of the Moral Majority in 1979 and of other groups later on, with their opposition to the 1973 abortion rights ruling of the Supreme Court, and strong defense of "traditional" family life) and even Midwestern conservatism, among others.[13] Former liberals, indeed former Trotskyites, became neo-conservatives in their concern to defeat communism and spread democracy. Their attitudes on big government did not necessarily endear them to traditionalists or libertarians. (Irving Kristol, the founding father of neoconservatism famously endorsed the welfare state and saw the role of those who agreed with him "to convert the Republican Party and American conservatism in general, against their respective wills, into a new kind of conservative politics suitable to governing a modern democracy."[14]) The religious right focused on moral issues that many other conservatives ultimately embraced, but did not fit well with libertarian doctrine. Later, so-called "big-government" or "compassionate" conservatives in the George W. Bush administration endorsed an expansion of Medicare to include a major drug benefit, while also insinuating the federal government ever deeper into education at the elementary and secondary level. They also put forth an expansive view of executive power that should have given pause to many more traditional conservatives.

But the point for now is that reactions to what many considered the radical movements of the sixties that changed many aspects of American life (and especially in the South to the effective enfranchisement of African Americans as a result of the Voting Rights Act of 1965), to humiliating defeat in Vietnam, and to Supreme Court decisions like Roe v. Wade in 1973 allowed conservatives, over time, the opportunity to build a political coalition that has transformed American politics. It has not been easy, and because of the complexities of contemporary conservatism, not been consistent, but conservatism today sits astride American politics in a way that few after the overwhelming defeat of Goldwater in 1964 thought possible.

Some Brief Post-1964 Political History

In 1968, Richard Nixon narrowly won the presidency in a three-person race. His "Southern strategy" in particular and his attempt to appeal to "the silent majority," were initial efforts to take advantage of the turmoil in the country and to transform the political landscape. While Nixon's huge triumph in the 1972 election was soon offset by reactions to the Watergate scandal and his subsequent resignation, the electoral success of Nixon's overall political strategy did not go unnoticed.

After unsuccessfully challenging President Ford for the Republican nomination in 1976, Ronald Reagan secured the nomination in 1980. His overall approach (despite the somewhat incongruous challenge to a sitting president of his own party) meshed well with notions about fusionism in conservative circles – Reagan popularized the notion of an Eleventh Commandment – speak no evil of a fellow Republican. Reagan did well with conservatives of all stripes, appealing to each of the strands of American conservatism with his virulent anti-communism, his endorsement of free markets, his public stand on abortion (perhaps a bit incongruous in light of his record in California, but such is the way in politics), and his very strong Southern strategy. On the latter, just after securing the Republican nomination in August 1980, Reagan gave a speech in Philadelphia, Mississippi (site of one of the most heinous crimes against civil rights workers in 1964) endorsing states' rights. Though the speech is rarely mentioned today, the venue and content must have sent a clear signal to Reagan's southern backers.

Following some ups and downs, conservatives scored a major triumph in 1994 when the Republican Party won control of both the House and the Senate. The House vote was especially significant in light of the national campaign run by Newt Gingrich on the basis of a set of proposals called the Contract with America. These proposals reflected many parts of the broad conservative agenda, including a balanced budget/tax limitation amendment, an anti-crime package with "effective death penalty provisions," a "personal responsibility act" limiting welfare, an act to prevent US troops from coming under UN command, and similar provisions.[15] With the 1994 congressional elections, the Republicans held a majority of House and Senate seats in the states of the old Confederacy, a remarkable accomplishment compared to the huge majorities the Democrats held after the 1964 elections in these states and the more than two-thirds of the seats that the Democrats still held in 1972.

Self-proclaimed "compassionate conservative" George W. Bush became president in 2001, following the disputed 2000 election. Compassionate, as Steven Teles points out, is not an adjective one would use in describing the Republican Party or its philosophy prior to 2000.[16] Indeed, as Teles says, "Conservative Republicans argued that Democratic compassion created the mess the nation had fallen into and threatened white working- and middle-class voters' recent, tenuous status in American society. Conservatives – both the shapers of the party's ideas and the crafters of its electoral appeals – attacked the idea of social justice, challenged the legitimacy of the modern administrative state, and rarely tried to claim that conservative ideas could aid the nation's poorer, blacker citizens." What Bush was attempting to do was bring together religious conservatives who accepted notions about serving the poor, those who believed that volunteerism, private charity and government assistance could be melded or complement one another in efforts to better society, and those who were willing to use a variety of mechanisms (including government) to produce desired outcomes. He combined this with tax cutting, leaving it for future administrations to deal with the consequences of increased deficits. Teles argues that the compassionate conservative approach ultimately failed politically within many Republican circles because it was seen to have "weakened the party's immune system against assault from the virus of big government." Whether success or failure in the United States, what David Cameron, the Conservative Party Prime Minister of the United Kingdom calls "modern compassionate conservatism" is still alive (if not altogether well) in Britain, where one can see it as a descendent of the type of conservatism Patten (see above) argued for.[17] I'll return to this in a later chapter (8) comparing conservatism in the UK and the United States.

It is also important to record the Bush administration's adoption of neo-conservative foreign policy ideas, especially after the September 11, 2001 terrorist attacks on the United States. The aggressive nation-building ideas the administration accepted would have seemed rather undesirable to the likes of Robert Taft half a century or more ago, and the aggressive notions about the "unitary executive" endorsed and adopted by the administration would have seemed simply beyond the pale

In short, what looked like disaster for conservatives and Republicans in 1964 and 1965 was the impetus for a period of political success. The losing Goldwater campaign left behind an inspired cadre that provided many of the activists for future campaigns. The negative reaction of white Southerners (and, to a lesser extent the reaction of others in the rest of the nation) to the civil rights laws, and especially the Voting Rights Act, passed as part of the Great Society, ate away at the foundation of the Democratic Party, with the Wallace movement and its attacks on liberalism undermining the voting strength of liberalism in the North. Abortion politics and the growing and more general relationship of religiosity to conservatism further increased the strength of the conservative movement. The Vietnam War and reactions to it by demonstrations and counter-culture figures repelled many people and created a distrust of government that has been a special boon to US conservatives.

Putting it all together, the Southern strategy, intense anti-communism, courting (and, no doubt, helping to create) what came to be called the religious right, with its opposition to abortion and support of traditional values in areas such as marriage and the family, skepticism about government programs and about government's role in the economy, cutting taxes, and a highly nationalistic and militarized foreign policy have yielded many political victories for those on the right. One indication of conservative success is that Republican politicians of all types tend to embrace the term "conservative" as a matter of course (and political survival within Republican ranks), while non-centrist Democrats often look for synonyms for "liberal" to describe themselves.

What I Endeavor to Do in This Book

My aim in this book is to examine whether or not the contemporary United States is a conservative nation, and, if it is a conservative nation, why that has come about and what that has come to mean. As I've noted above, there is no accepted definition of "conservative" in the US. Rather, there are numerous strands of thought that often overlap and sometimes conflict. It is pointless, in my view, to argue about what real conservatism is. That is obviously in the eye of the beholder, shaped by previous thought and experience and by the political issues and experiences of the day. One thing one can do in a relatively systematic and objective way is to look at how people designate themselves (do they call themselves conservatives, moderates, or liberals?), and to examine what attitudes and behaviors go with the designation they choose. One could go further and try to isolate combinations of attitudes and behaviors that go with a term such as conservative, but given the complexity of the issues that is likely to yield complex typologies. That can be a useful endeavor, but my main goal here is to take a broader brush to what we know is often a loose coalition of those with different, and sometimes contradictory or non-complementary, passions and to consider the correlates and implications of the views that mark conservatism in the US. The emphasis is on the views of the public – particularly what it means for people to call themselves conservatives and what impact that has on their political behavior – but this will be examined against a background of social and institutional forces and, at times later in the book, in comparison to the views of elites.

Chapter 2 jumps right into the question of whether or not the United States is a conservative nation, or, better, whether the population thinks of itself as conservative. The short answer is that self-identified conservatives have been the modal (largest, most frequent) group in the country for some time, though not quite a majority. The chapter then examines the tightening of the relationship between conservatism and Republican Party identification in the United States, a process that is most marked in the South and that has transformed American politics over the past half century. And it has short sections focusing on those who say they "don't know" or "haven't thought about it" when asked to identify themselves as liberals or conservatives, as well as on the views of African Americans.

Chapter 3 looks at who the conservatives are in the mass public. Who are the people who call themselves conservatives? Where do they come from? Is there anything that stands out about them with respect to gender, marital status or age? What types of families do they come from? Do they tend to be younger or older than the general population? What are their religious and social beliefs? And what is the political significance of those beliefs?

Chapter 4 continues the examination of who the conservatives are by focusing on the beliefs about economic issues and the size and role of government of people who call themselves conservatives. In what ways do conservatives differ from others in the public in their opinions on these issues? What is the significance of the fact that many conservatives in the general public support key elements of the welfare state in fact, though they reject the welfare state in principle?

Chapter 5 focuses on changes over time. The emphasis is on comparing 1972 data to data collected in later election years, especially in 2008 and 2012. Nineteen seventy-two was chosen because it was the first year where the American National Election Study (ANES), a major source of the data I use in this book, asked people to self-identify as conservatives or liberals and because it was a year that was still a part of what we roughly call the sixties. Two thousand and eight and 2012 were the years of the last full ANES election studies available for analysis at the time the book was written.

Chapter 6 turns to elites and examines conservatism among political and administrative leaders. It uses a unique data set to compare the views of political elites to those of the general public, focusing on comparisons of political polarization within each group.

Chapter 7 looks at the Tea Party movement in the United States that swept to prominence with its successes in the "wave election" of 2010. The focus is on the significance of Tea Party sympathizers in terms of how their views on political issues compare to the views of others. The analysis in the chapter confirms that Tea Party adherents are mainly very conservative Republicans, and that they turn out in large numbers to vote in primaries and caucuses. As a result, they have disproportionate influence in choosing nominees and also have the potential, often realized, to reinforce the tendency of their representatives to support positions that create problems in basic areas such as keeping the government running.

Chapter 8 takes up the issue raised in Chapter 1 about the meaning of conservatism. The focus is on a comparative analysis of the strategies and approaches of conservatives in the United Kingdom and the United States and on the varieties of conservatism in the US. The chapter points up a dilemma of US conservatism, namely that it is big enough to compete regularly and to win control of parts of government (House, Senate or the Presidency) often enough so that it always looks formidable, and therefore its representatives and supporters have less incentive than their counterparts in the United Kingdom to adapt and change. The chapter also briefly lays out the varieties of conservatism among US conservative elites, an area that often divides the activists in the movement.

Chapter 9 brings it all together. It argues that while in many ways conservatism is now highly influential and often appears triumphant – in the size of its group of adherents and in the strong beliefs and activism of many of them, in its vibrant organizational structures, in its consolidation of the South as a dominant wing of the Republican Party, just to take a few examples – there are also numerous weaknesses. A significant part of the conservative constituency in the mass public wants to retain government programs such as Social Security at or above current levels of expenditure and has also gradually accepted, though often grudgingly or incompletely, many of the cultural and social changes that the sixties activists fought for. The upheavals of the 1960s made possible an African American president of a moderate conservative nation, but these same upheavals also stimulated the fierce elite divisions and often passionate and activist conservative base that now make US politics highly conflictual. The immediate future for conservatism is clearly strong because of the great strength of the conservative brand in the general public, the robust institutional structure of conservative organizations and media, and the favorable effects for conservative prospects as a result of redistricting after the 2010 election. Over the long term, however, demographic and value changes will likely make it difficult to maintain the level of support conservatism has enjoyed over the last half century.

Endnotes

1 "Our Mission Statement," November 19, 1955, See www.nationalreview.com/.

2 See Congressional Budget Office, "Revenues, Outlays, Deficits, Surplus, and Debt Held by the Public, 1971 to 2010, in Billions of Dollars," Table, E-1, www.cbo.gov.

3 George Nash, *The Conservative Intellectual Movement in America Since 1945* (Wilmington: ISI Books, 2006), page xviii.

4 The phrases and quoted material in the last three paragraphs are from Samuel Huntington, "Conservatism as an Ideology," *American Political Science Review*, Vol. 51, No. 2 (June, 1957), pages 454–457. For a "bare-boned" rendering of the principles of the Conservative tradition, see Clinton Rossiter, *Conservatism in America: The Thankless Persuasion"* (New York: Knopf, 1962), pages 64–66.

5 Chris Patten, *The Tory Case* (London: Longman, 1983), page 3.

6 Patten, *The Tory Case* (1983), page 17, quoting E. Burke, *Reflections on the Revolution in France* (Penguin Classics), page 267. For an interesting recent biography of Burke, see Jesse Norman, *Edmund Burke: The First Conservative* (New York: Basic Books, 2013).

7 Patten, *The Tory Case* (1983), page 2.

8 See James T. Patterson, *Mr. Republican: A Biography of Robert Taft* (Boston: Houghton Mifflin, 1972). The description of Taft as an isolationist and opponent of executive dominance of foreign policy can be found on pages 196–197 of Patterson and the quotation from Taft is on page 437.

9 The abstractions quote is from Patterson (1972), page 41, and the other quoted phrases are from pages 320 and 615.

10 Lee Edwards, "The Conservative Consensus," http://www.heritage.org/research/reports/2007/01/the-conservative-consensus-frank-meyer-barry-goldwater-and-the-politics-of-fusionism, page 1.

11 George H. Nash, "Conservatism on Center Stage," in Charles W. Dunn, ed., *The Future of Conservatism: Conflict and Consensus in the Post-Reagan Era* (Wilmington: ISI Books, 2007), page 7.

12 Theodore H. White, *The Making of the President, 1964* (New York: Atheneum, 1965).

13 Dunn, 2007, "Introduction: Conservatism on Center Stage," pages vii–viii.

14 Irving Kristol, "The Neoconservative Persuasion," *The Weekly Standard*, August 25, 2003, http://www.weeklystandard.com/the-neoconservative-persuasion/article/4246.

15 *Contract with America*, 1994, http://www.nationalcenter.org/ContractwithAmerica.html, accessed 05/03/16.

16 Steven Teles, "Compassionate Conservatism, Domestic Policy, and the Politics of Ideational Change," pp. 178–211 in Joel D. Aberbach and Gillian Peele, eds., *Crisis of Conservatism? The Republican Party, the Conservative Movement and American Politics After Bush* (New York: Oxford University Press, 2011).

17 The quoted phrases are from Teles, "Compassionate Conservatism" (2011), pages 180, 205 and 207.

2 Is the United States a Conservative Nation?

The simple answer to the question in the title to this chapter is something like "not quite, but close to it." Certainly, as we shall see, it is fair to say that self-defined conservatives are the modal group in the general public, that is the largest group in the triumvirate of conservatives, liberals and moderates (and larger also than people who cannot or will not classify themselves in these terms). But it was not always so that people who call themselves conservatives were the largest group of the three in the US, and the story of how the change occurred is the key to understanding the nature of contemporary conservatism in the United States.

A Change in the 1960s

Measuring public opinion about liberalism and conservatism goes back to the 1930s. Data from surveys available through the Roper Center for Public Opinion Research, drawn from numerous surveys done prior to 1972, when a question on ideological self-identification became a standard part of the American National Election Studies (ANES), indicates that the public was probably evenly split between liberals and conservatives from 1936 to 1965. Of the 18 available surveys in the Roper Center collection in this period (using a variety of measures), eight showed more liberals than conservatives, eight indicated more conservatives than liberals and two were tied. In short, as Christopher Ellis and James Stimson conclude from the same data in their 2012 book on *Ideology in America*, the liberal identification was, as far as we can discern, not dominant among the US public in the period that one would think was the heyday of liberalism, though it clearly was every bit as common as conservative identification.[1]

Post-1965, however, the story changes: All 17 relevant surveys from Roper with indicators of public identification with liberalism or conservatism in the period post-1965 and ending in 1971 show more conservatives than liberals. And in every year starting in 1976 the ANES surveys consistently show more conservatives than liberals. So something happened in the second half of the 1960s to change things, and the change has lasted.

What I will do in the rest of this chapter is examine the ANES data starting in 1972, looking at its consistency, exceptions that may exist among major racial groups, and changes in the relationship between the liberal/conservative measure (what I will also call the ideology measure in the book) and another fundamental indicator of political identification in the US – identification as a Republican or a Democrat – to understand the changing political significance of a person describing himself or herself as a political conservative or liberal. The latter is meant, among other things, to begin addressing a lingering question about the type of survey data I am discussing here, namely, how significant is it? Are people who identify as conservatives or liberals in public opinion surveys merely taking a symbolic stance, often unrelated to other views one might expect them to hold, or is there more to it than that? If so, has the substance or importance of conservative identification changed over time, and what does that mean for American politics

Measuring Ideology

We are fortunate to have a measure of liberalism–conservatism that has been used by the American National Election Studies since 1972. Respondents are asked a simple question: "Where would you place yourself on this scale, or haven't you thought much about it?: Extremely Liberal; Liberal; Slightly Liberal; Moderate, Middle of the Road; Slightly Conservative; Conservative; Extremely Conservative." (The 2010 ANES used a slightly modified scale: Very Liberal; Somewhat Liberal; Closer to Liberals; Neither; Closer to Conservatives: Somewhat Conservative; Very Conservative.) The seven-point scale is straight-forward and, at one level, unambiguous. We know from their answers how people perceive their own positions in terms of liberalism or conservatism. What we do not know, of course, is what precisely they think these terms mean. The answers, in other words, are purely subjective. However, those who have not thought at all about whether or not they are conservatives or liberals are invited to tell that to the interviewer (and others are free to refuse to answer). What the measure gives us is a simple scale that we can track through time that is, at the same time, a measure we can relate to other measures to probe in greater depth the characteristics of people who call themselves conservative or liberal and also what they think about a variety of issues or questions.

Is the Scale Reliable and Valid?

Fortunately, the available data allow for a good test of reliability. The scale was administered twice in recent ANES surveys, once before the election and then again after the election was held. Keeping in mind that some people might legitimately change their minds over the course of a

Table 2.1 Pre-Election x Post-Election Answers to the Ideology Question, All Respondents, 2012

| | Post-Election Measure | | | | | | | | | |
Pre-Election Measure	Extremely Liberal	Liberal	Slightly Liberal	Moderate	Slightly Conservative	Conservative	Extremely Conservative	Row Totals	(Weighted N=)	Row Percentages
Extremely Liberal	55.2	23.0	8.0	9.8	0.0	2.3	1.7	100.0	(155.8)	3.2
Liberal	4.8	69.8	14.9	9.1	0.7	0.6	0.1	100.0	(540.0)	11.1
Slightly Liberal	1.0	14.1	52.2	25.3	5.1	1.8	0.4	100.0	(571.2)	11.7
Moderate	0.6	3.5	10.4	70.1	11.4	3.8	0.3	100.0	(1,665.1)	33.8
Slightly Conservative	0.2	1.9	6.1	23.1	49.5	18.4	0.8	100.0	(780.2)	15.9
Conservative	0.2	0.1	1.7	6.5	10.1	75.5	5.9	100.0	(957.8)	19.6
Extremely Conservative	2.3	1.3	1.3	5.3	5.9	24.0	59.8	100.0	(230.8)	4.7
										100

Gamma = .84

Weighted N = 4,894.9
Unweighted N = 4,761

Data source: ANES 2012

Question wording:

Ideology measure: Where would you place YOURSELF on this scale, or haven't you thought much about this? Extremely Liberal; Liberal; Slightly Liberal; Moderate; Middle of the Road; Slightly Conservative; Conservative; Extremely Conservative.

few months, that is, not through ignorance, but because of exposure to various arguments, the consistency of answers received is stunning.

Take 2012 as an example, the correlation (gamma[2]) between answers to the question asking respondents whether they are conservatives or liberals – I'll regularly term this the ideology question in the book – are quite consistent. A look at Table 2.1 shows that the correlation between the respondents' pre-election and post-election answers to the ideology question is a very robust .84. Very few respondents shifted from conservative to liberal or vice versa between the surveys; what little movement exists is within categories of liberal or conservative, and even that is almost always across a single category of the response, for example, between "Extremely Liberal" and "Liberal" or "Extremely Conservative" and "Conservative." Also note that the "extreme" categories, not surprisingly given the connotation of the word "extreme," are relatively small.

When it comes to validity, aside from the obvious "face validity" of the item, that is the question appears on the face of it to measure what it is meant to measure, the data, as analyzed, will themselves be further evidence of the measure's validity. The relationships of the ideology measure with other (outside) variables are such that most readers should be convinced that the variable is a meaningful measure of conservative/liberal self-identification and not just a set of relatively meaningless responses to a stimulus.

Conservatism since 1972

Figure 2.1 is a simple presentation of the percentage of respondents in each survey year who describe themselves as either slightly conservative, conservative, or extremely conservative. What a glance at the figure shows immediately is that the percentage of people who call themselves conservative has hovered near the 40 percent mark for the time that the question has been asked (the overall mean is 41.1 percent and the standard deviation is 3.36), with a low of 35.7 in 1974 and highs of 46.8 in 1994 (the year that conservative Republicans swept to power in the off-year elections) and 48.2 in 2010 (another "wave" election for the Republicans, although the slight change in the question form may also account for some of the increase). Basically, there hasn't been a great deal of variation over the time period covered, with perhaps a slight consolidation of conservative identification starting in 1980.

Beyond that, and not visible in this figure, the percentage of liberals is generally about 26, and the balance of the population (about 33 percent) are self-described moderates. In short, self-described conservatives of various stripes share domination of the political landscape with self-described moderates, while liberals are the smallest group in this triumvirate with about a quarter of the population using some form of this label to describe themselves.[3] The pre-1966 political landscape, certainly

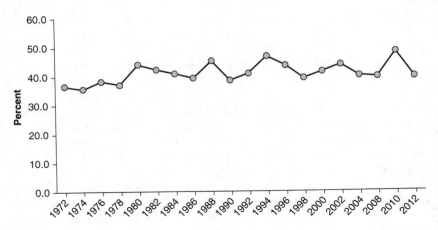

Figure 2.1 Percent Conservative, by Year, 1972–2012 (All Respondents)

Data Source: 1972–2012 ANES. Weighted data used in years where weights appropriate

Conservative = respondents choosing Slightly Conservative, Conservative, or Extremely Conservative.

<u>Question wording</u>:
Ideology measure: Where would you place YOURSELF on this scale, or haven't you thought much about this? Extremely Liberal; Liberal; Slightly Liberal; Moderate; Middle of the Road; Slightly Conservative; Conservative; Extremely Conservative. (For 2010: Very Liberal; Somewhat Liberal; Closer to Liberal; Neither; Closer to Conservative; Somewhat Conservative; Very Conservative).

when it comes to how people perceive themselves in terms of liberalism and conservatism, has undergone a decided change. The US population is now best characterized as, most commonly, either moderately conservative in its self-described political orientation – the "Slightly Conservative" and "Conservative" self-descriptions predominate, with "Extremely Conservative" usually 3 or 4 percent.

Wait a minute, you might say, there are segments of the US population – large demographic groups – that are liberal. And surely this is true, but it is less true of some of the larger categories we often use to characterize our population than one might think. If one looks, as I do in more detail in Chapter 3, at the ideology measure broken down by the broad racial or ethnic categories commonly used in contemporary social science, one finds that African Americans are the only group where liberals are modal (the most common group), and even here, starting in the early 1980s, liberals just barely outnumber people who describe themselves as "Moderate, Middle of the Road." In all other groups, there are usually more self-described conservatives than moderates or liberals, although the margins are relatively small for Asians, Native Americans and Hispanics. African Americans alone are sufficiently unique to suggest separate analysis, a factor reinforced by the fact that in political terms African Americans have been so overwhelmingly Democratic in their party orientation and in voting in the modern period that most attempts to relate their party orientations or voting to something like the ideology measure yield no meaningful results. Therefore, from now on, unless clearly noted, I will consider the data with African Americans filtered out.[4]

In short, an average of about 41 percent of all Americans (43 percent without African Americans included in the analysis) have been describing themselves as conservatives of some type since at least the early 1970s. The question is how significant that is. Respondents may simply like the sound of the word conservative – it implies solidity, weighty judgment, a fondness for tradition, that sort of thing. Or they may, for some non-political reason, dislike the term liberal, confusing it with spendthrift, or immoral, or some other generally un-admired quality.[5]

However, examination of the over-time data will suggest a different story. Take, for example, the relationship, crucial for understanding the evolution of conservatism in the US, between a person's party identification (whether a person identifies with a political party and how strongly he or she feels that party identification to be – running from Strong Democrat through Independent at the mid-point to Strong Republican) and his or her self-placement on the liberalism–conservatism scale. If the term conservatism lacks political meaning for a good part of the population most of the time, then it should have relatively little influence on what political scientists generally consider the most consistently meaningful political identification people in the United States have – their identification with one of the two major parties.[6]

But when we take a look, we see a meaningful string of relationships that tells an important tale about ideology in the United States since 1972, and about the impact of the conflicts that have gripped American politics in recent times. Table 2.2 shows the relationship of party identification to placement on the ideology measure starting in 1972, with region controlled (that is, separately for those living in the 11 states of the old Confederacy – what I'll now simply call the South,[7] and for those living in other parts of the country – the Non-South, or North, in the shorthand I'll use). The measure used to show the relationship is a simple one called "gamma" which, in our case, tells us whether the ordering (rank) a respondent chooses on one measure (party identification) is associated with the ordering (rank) chosen on a second variable (in our case, conservatism). A correlation of +1.0 equals perfect association (agreement), so that respondents always agreed on the rank order, and a correlation of −1.0 means a perfectly negative association (complete disagreement). Zero means no relationship. So, for example, a perfect relationship (1.0) would tell us that anyone who identified as a "Extremely Conservative" was also surely coded as "Strong Republican."[8]

The South (Old Confederacy)/Non-South (North) regional breakdown is used because of the historical impact of the Civil War on party identification in the South. White Southerners controlled politics and, in

Table 2.2 Correlations (Gamma) between Ideology and Party ID, by Region, 1972–2012

Year	South*	Non-South
1972	.15	.35
1974	.22	.36
1976	.26	.39
1978	.32	.35
1980	.34	.40
1982	.35	.49
1984	.29	.46
1986	.24	.42
1988	.36	.46
1990	.29	.39
1992	.38	.45
1994	.45	.55
1996	.56	.57
1998	.47	.51
2000	.45	.48
2002	.50	.55
2004	.63	.67
2008	.63	.64
2010	.61	.66
2012	.63	.66

Grouped Means		
Year	South*	Non-South
1972–1991	.29	.41
1994–2002	.49	.53
2004–2012	.63	.66

Data source: 1972–2012 ANES. Weighted data used in years where weights appropriate
Note: African American respondents filtered out.

* South = the 11 secession states.

Question wording:
Ideology Measure: See Figure 2.1 note.

Party ID: Generally speaking, do you usually think of yourself as a [DEMOCRAT, a REPUBLICAN/a REPUBLICAN, a DEMOCRAT], an INDEPENDENT, or what? Would you call yourself a STRONG [Democrat/Republican] or a NOT VERY STRONG [Democrat/Republican]? (Recoded to: Strong Democrat; Not Very Strong Democrat; Independent Democrat; Independent; Independent Republican; Not Very Strong Republican; Strong Republican.).

most cases identified as Democrats, no matter who the party's candidate for president might be or how the candidate's views correlated with their own. In fact, in these states, the most important electoral contest tended to be the Democratic primary.[9] What this meant was that identification as a Democrat, in the absence of a better indicator of liberalism/conservatism, suggested little about the political views of Southern respondents. And, in general, people could easily be confused about the ideological implications of being a Democrat since most white southerners identified as Democrats no matter what their other political beliefs might be.

The data show a revealing pattern. The correlation between party identification and ideology was moderately strong in the North in 1972, but relatively weak in the South. (A positive coefficient in this table indicates that conservatives tend to be Republicans and liberals tend to be Democrats.) The relationship grew stronger in the South in 1974 and held fairly steady (though with a noticeable upward trend) until 1994. It then arched upward until it reached high points in the South in 2004 through 2012. In the North, the relationship also tended roughly upward after 1994, also reaching high points in 2004, 2010 and 2012. In fact, beginning in 1994 the relationships are almost exactly the same in the North and South and the strength of the relationships increased starting in 2004 to the point where they are remarkably strong given that we are using survey data.

Table 2.3 illustrates much of the story. It shows the percent of conservatives, Southern and Northern, who identified as Republicans in the presidential election years from 1972 to 2012.[10] While the percentage of Northern conservatives who were Republicans was relatively high in every year (though greatest in the years starting in 2004, as one might suspect from Table 2.2), there was a marked increase over time in the South in the percentage of conservatives who identified as Republicans. In 1972 only 39 percent of Southerners who identified as conservatives also identified as Republicans, but by 2004 that figure topped 80 percent (and stayed close to that thereafter). In essence, by 2004 ideological politics – using that shorthand label here for a confluence of placement on the liberalism–conservatism scale and party identification – was the same throughout the country. In that sense, the Southern anomaly had disappeared. A process had been completed in which the South was just like the rest of the country, only, at least for the non-black population we've been focusing on here, just a wee bit more Republican within ideological categories. American politics was now quite different than it had been in the period coming out of the long 1960s decade that came to a close in the early 1970s: it was not that conservative identification had increased, but people had sorted themselves out so that conservative and Republican went together much more clearly than the two had earlier.

Table 2.3 Percent of Conservatives* Who Identify as Republicans, by Region, 1972–2012

Year	South **	Non-South
1972	39.2	63.7
1976	46.0	67.0
1980	52.2	63.4
1984	60.9	73.7
1988	63.8	72.8
1992	70.3	67.7
1996	74.4	74.3
2000	79.0	66.1
2004	87.0	85.6
2008	83.6	78.8
2010	78.5	79.9
2012	81.7	79.1

Data source: 1972–2012 ANES
Note: African American respondents filtered out.

*Conservatives include respondents choosing Slightly Conservative, Conservative, or Extremely Conservative on the 7-point scale. (For 2010, Republicans include Strong Republicans, Not Very Strong Republicans, and Independent Republicans).
**South = the 11 secession states.

Question wording:
See Figure 2.1.

How did this come about? Clearly, there was some significant changing of party identification in the population (see below), particularly in the South, to bring it and professed conservatism (which did not change much) into such close alignment. And it is also likely, though to a lesser extent given the stability in the percentages of conservatives over the time period, that some people changed their identification as conservatives or liberals to fit their party identification.[11] What matters, for the moment, is that when the smoke cleared, the United States had two parties whose constituencies were much more clear-cut than they had been before: one party (the Republicans) had adherents who were much more likely to identify as conservatives than the other, and regional disparities in the relationship between party and conservatism had disappeared.

And, further, the fact that the changing pattern of relationships was most prominent in the South, and that the changes followed so soon after the emergence of a formidable African American vote in the South brought about by the Voting Rights Act of the mid-1960s and then the emergence of the Religious Right in the early 1970s following Roe v. Wade and the Carter administration's efforts to tax Southern academies designed to circumvent integration, is clearly more than coincidence. Events and decisions by elected officials changed the political reality so significantly that people slowly brought their party identifications much more strongly into line than they had been before with their ideological self-identifications. This process was more pronounced in the South, which was still majority Democratic in party identification in 1972 (tilting to majority Republican by 2002), because the core issues that caused the changes had the greatest impact in the South and the Democratic identification of Southerners and were so deeply entwined with the history and sense of grievance there, but it also occurred in the North as a growing sense – and, clearly, reality – took hold that the Republican Party was a vehicle for conservatism.

Buttressing this argument is that although it took a while for conservatism and party identification to fall in line, there was no such lag in voting. The North and South look remarkably alike when it comes to the relationship between conservatism and voting in presidential elections, at least since the first year (1972) where we have measures of both in the American National Election Studies.[12] The correlation between the two in that year is .63 in the North and .64 in the South, and the two regions show a similar pattern in presidential elections through 1988. (The average correlations between the conservatism measure and the vote is .62 in the North and .59 in the South, with only one slightly deviant year – 1984 – where the correlation is .44 in the South.) Then, starting in 1992 the average correlation rises to .78 in the South and .83 in the North, with the coefficients in both regions usually well above .80 starting in 2004. It was clearly easier for (white) Southerners to bring their voting behavior into line with their beliefs than to give up their traditional party identification, but eventually those who identified as conservatives were also much more likely to identify themselves as Republicans.

Briefly, whether or not a respondent considered himself or herself a conservative mattered a lot for how that person voted in presidential elections (with conservatives voting for the Republican candidate) starting at least in 1972, even though it took the relationship between whether the person identified as a Republican or Democrat (Party Identification) some time to catch up, a process especially marked in the South, but present throughout the country. In 1972 conservatives across the nation, especially in the South, were in large part voting Republican but they were not necessarily calling themselves Republicans. By 2012 conservatives throughout the nation were not only voting Republican but, as we saw in Table 2.3, they were very likely to identify as Republicans as well. Put the other way around, the South had gone from almost 50 percent of solid conservatives (those describing themselves as "Extremely Conservative" or "Conservative") who identified as "Strong Democrat" or "Leaning Democrat" to 5 percent, now mirroring the rest of the country in this respect. In fact, by 2008, the South had gone from less than 30 percent Republican identifiers to over 50 percent, while Republican strength in the rest of the country remained basically the same (around 40 percent).[13] The Republican Party, which once had been a minority voice in the South, was now the major partisan force there (with the most notable exception being the large African American population – see the next section).

To sum up, while many (non-black) Southern voters may once have called themselves Democrats, they had been identifying themselves as conservatives and voting for Republican candidates for many years. But as the years passed, the labels conservative and Republican became tied closely together in ways they had not been before, a process particularly striking in the South because the relationship between the two was once much weaker there. Thus, by 2012 (the latest data in the ANES series analyzed for this book), the terms "conservative" and "Republican" were, it could be said, "joined at the hip" throughout the nation and the South was, through this change, transformed from an uneasy base of the Democratic Party to a more comfortable base for the Republican Party.

What about the African Americans?

As expected, African Americans are the least conservative major demographic group in the United States. However, that does not mean that African Americans overwhelmingly identify as liberals. What the data show is that in the surveys taken from 1972 to 2012, African Americans

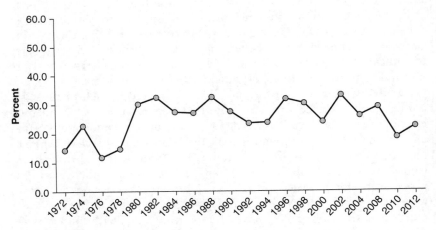

Figure 2.2 Percent Conservative, African American Respondents, by Year, 1972–2012

Data Source: 1972–2012 ANES. Weighted data used in years where weights appropriate

Conservative = respondents choosing Slightly Conservative, Conservative, or Extremely Conservative.

<u>Question wording</u>:
Ideology measure: See Figure 2.1 note.

were equally likely to identify as moderates or middle of the road (an average of about 37 percent) as they were to call themselves liberals (also 37 percent), with about 26 percent identifying as conservatives. This shifted slightly in 2012, with the moderate category gaining about 6 points (to 43 percent) and liberals dropping slightly to 35 percent. Overall, while a liberal identification is much more common among African Americans than among whites, it is effectively tied with (and perhaps slightly behind) identification as a moderate or middle of the road identification and only about 11 percent more likely than a conservative identification. Put another way, while significantly fewer African Americans call themselves conservatives than is the case for whites (or Hispanics), an average of about a quarter of African Americans surveyed who have an ideological self-identification call themselves conservatives (see Figure 2.2).

What is different in this regard about African Americans, as noted above, is that ideological identification and both party identification and vote choice is, to put it mildly, much less tightly coupled. The reason is simple: No matter what their ideological position, over 80 percent of African Americans identify as Democrats of some type (Strong Democrat to Independent Democrat) and this has been the case for some time, and the percentage of African Americans voting for Democratic presidential candidates has been about 90 percent or better in the period when the ANES conservatism measure is available (i.e. starting in 1972). As a result, there is relatively little to say about the relationship between conservatism and partisanship or vote for African Americans because people in this demographic identify with and vote for the Democrats regardless of their other political views.[14] Republicans, with their "Southern strategy," have lost much of the 30 percent of the black vote they received as late as 1960.

This is not to say that there are no useful predictors of who among African Americans identify as conservatives. Religiosity, for example, is a factor (though in correlational terms not as important as among the rest of the population), one I will take up later in the book in a more general way, but well worth probing in any analysis focusing on conservatism among blacks.

A Note about the "Don't Knows" and "Haven't Thought Much about Its"

So far we have been looking at the views of people who make a choice and place themselves somewhere on the conservative–liberal scale. But what about those who do not place themselves, who say that they "don't know" or "haven't thought about it much"?

For the years 1972–2012, in years when responses such as "don't know" and "haven't thought about it" were recorded, an average of about 28 percent of all respondents fell into these categories. The figures are somewhat lower for the years 2000–2012, about 23 percent, but still quite high.[15] African Americans were the most likely to give such responses (about 44 percent) for reasons that will be made clear below. But what is also clear is that at least a quarter of the American population as a whole cannot or will not choose a position on the scale.

However, and it's a big however, when the people who choose "don't know" or "haven't thought about it" are asked to choose whether they are liberals, moderates or conservatives (something done in most of the surveys starting in 1984, though not in 2010), they chose Conservative over other categories in every year but 1998 and 2000. And in years when Moderates were asked the follow-up question, they also showed a tendency to prefer the conservative label more than the liberal label (in 7 of the 9 years for which we have data). My point is not that these people were surely conservative, but that the label, at minimum, has a tendency to be the more popular one.

Not surprisingly, when one digs a bit deeper and looks at exactly who these people who answer "don't know" or "haven't thought about it," a few facts stand out. They are less likely to be registered to vote than those who made an initial choice in answering the question. They are also less likely than others to vote even if they are registered. They are hugely overrepresented among people who have only completed grade school, and less so, but still very significantly, among those who completed high school. In short, they are among the least educated or least politically active segments of the population. In this sense at least, they have relatively less influence on politics and disproportionately come from the segments of American society that are least advantaged educationally. When it comes to the latter, that is, deprivation in terms of levels of education, it is hardly a surprise that the African American population has more people proportionately who are in the "don't know" or "haven't thought about it" categories. It is also the case that when it comes to examining the ideological views of Americans, focusing on those who are at least minimally able to articulate such views – by answering a survey question – is the sensible way to proceed. But it is important to keep in the back of one's mind when digesting data on conservatism or liberalism in the US that there are many people who are extraordinarily uninvolved in the debate, although even among these people there is apparently more sympathy for the term conservative than for the term liberal.

Endnotes

1 Christopher Ellis and James A. Stimson, *Ideology in America* (New York: Cambridge University Press, 2012), pages 68–72.
2 "Goodman and Kruskal's gamma (G or γ) is a nonparametric measure of the strength and direction of association that exists between two variables measured on an ordinal scale. Whilst it is possible to analyse such data using Spearman's rank-order correlation or Kendall's tau-b, Goodman and

Kruskal's gamma is recommended when your data has many tied ranks." https://statistics.laerd.com/spss-tutorials/goodman-and-kruskals-gamma-using-spss-statistics.php

3 The three categories of liberals, when added together, have the smallest standard deviation (2.67). Most of the tradeoffs in the series are between the moderate and conservative labels.

4 For some comparable data from a different study and a similar analytic decision, see Joel D. Aberbach, "The Future of the American Right," especially p. 47 in Joel D. Aberbach and Gillian Peele, eds., *Crisis of Conservatism? The Republican Party, the Conservative Movement, and American Politics After Bush* (New York: Oxford University Press, 2011).

5 See Christopher Ellis and James A. Stimson, *Ideology in America* (2012), especially pages 124–145.

6 The complex exception in the US is the historically strong regional effect on identification with the Democratic Party. The change in that effect over the last half century is part of the story of the rise of ideologically polarized politics in the US and is the focal point of this section of Chapter 2.

7 The states of the Confederacy were: Alabama, Arkansas, Florida, Georgia, Louisiana, Mississippi, North Carolina, South Carolina, Tennessee, Texas, and Virginia.

8 See Note 2 above for a brief definition of the gamma statistic and its uses.

9 The classic work on Southern politics in this era is V.O. Key, *Southern Politics in State and Nation* (New York: Knopf, 1949).

10 An excellent treatment of this phenomenon in the North from 1972 to 1988 can be found in Edward G. Carmines and Harold W. Stanley, "The Transformation of the New Deal Party System: Social Groups, Political Ideology, and Changing Partisanship among Northen Whites, 1972–1988," *Political Behavior*, Vol. 14, No. 3 (1992), pages 213–237. A fine work on the partisan transformation of the South is David Lublin, *The Republican South: Democratization and Party Change* (Princeton: Princeton University Press, 2004). A very good overall summary of work on partisan polarization in congressional electoral politics can be found in Gary C. Jacobson, "Partisan Polarization in American Politics: A Background Paper," *Presidential Studies Quarterly*, Vol. 43, No. 4 (December 2013), pages 688–708.

11 See Robert D. Putnam and David E. Campbell, *American Grace: How Religion Divides and United Us* (New York: Simon and Schuster, 2010), especially page 145 on the dynamics of the "sorting out of political liberals into the secular camp and political conservatives into the highly religious camp."

12 Including third party candidates in the dependent variable – vote choice – in 1980 (Anderson), 1992 (Perot) and 1996 (Perot) lowers the relationships somewhat but does not impact the pattern described in the paragraph.

13 These figures were calculated using all three categories of Republican in the ANES measure of Party Identification: Strong Republican, Not Very Strong Republican, and Independent Republican.

14 This also holds at the congressional level, though to a slightly lesser extent. For example, in 2008 the relationship between the conservatism scale and partisan voting for Congress (Democratic candidate/Republican candidate) was .36 for African Americans, but .64 for Hispanics, .83 for whites, and 1.00 for the small number of Asians in the ANES sample.

15 In 2012 only face-to-face interviewees (about 35 percent of the total) were asked the follow-up question.

3 Who Are the Conservatives?

We know (from Chapter 2) that if one asks the typical American today whether he or she is a liberal, a moderate or a conservative, that more people are likely to choose some variant of conservative over other labels. And we know that this has been true for many years. Further, we have evidence suggesting that it has probably been the case since the mid-1960s that, of those making a choice, people have tended to choose the conservative as opposed to the liberal label to describe themselves. And we know that self-designating as a conservative has more and more become associated with being a Republican. We now turn to asking what other characteristics go with being a conservative. This chapter focuses mainly on demographic characteristics and social (including religious) beliefs; Chapter 4 focuses on the political beliefs of conservatives about the size and role of government.

Region

In Chapter 2 we examined one of the many political changes in the southern part of the United States since 1972: More and more non-African American southerners not only cast their votes for Republicans, but there is a stronger and stronger linking of the relationship between calling oneself a conservative and identifying as a Republican. One might therefore suppose that the South – and now I'm referring only to the part of the southern population that is not African American – has become more and more conservative over time.

However, this is decidedly not the case. The South – defined as the 11 states of the old Confederacy – was more conservative by about 12 percentage points than the rest of the country (the "North") in 1972 (48 percent to 36 percent) and only 7 percent more conservative in 2012 (47 percent to 40 percent). Both regions, then, saw small changes in conservatism in the survey data, with a slightly larger change in the North (a 4 percentage point increase in the North versus a 1 percentage point decrease in the South in self-identified conservatives), and the changes are too small to regard as significant.[1] The bottom line is that the South is consistently more conservative than the North, but the regional differences are modest. What marks the South off is that its conservatives have switched party allegiance to the point where the relationship between conservatism and party is the same in the North and the South and that there is now a tendency beyond that for more non-black southerners than non-black northerners to identify with the Republicans. (Social scientists would label this a change in the intercept if it was plotted on a series of regression equations.)

Gender, Marital Status and Age

As with region, there are noticeable but generally not very large differences in conservatism when one looks at various demographic groups, certainly when one looks at them in a simple and straightforward way.

Take gender, for example. Females are less conservative than males, but not by much. In 2008, for example, 43 percent of males identified as some type of conservative as opposed to 39 percent of females, and the figures are very similar in 2012 (45 percent of males versus 39 percent of females.). On the other end of the spectrum, 25 percent of males said they were liberals compared to 31 percent of females in 2008, with both sexes at 25 percent liberal in 2012.

Considering marital status, however, is more revealing. Married people are significantly more conservative than people who are not married. Again, looking at 2008 data, slightly more than half of currently married people (52 percent) describe themselves as some form of conservative, whereas only 29 percent of those who have never been married call themselves conservative. Divorced people are closer to the unmarried than the married, with 37 percent identifying as conservative, while widowed individuals look more like those who are married, with 49 percent identifying as conservative. Since a little over 60 percent of the sample is either married or widowed, conservatives have a clear edge, but the trend away from marriage is likely to diminish the conservative advantage in the future. The same basic results were found in 2012.[2]

Incidentally, these findings on marital status hold for men as well as for women, though men tend to be slightly more conservative than women within marital categories.

Age is meaningful, but not the huge predictor of conservatism one might have thought. In the 2008 data, about 48 percent of those who were born before 1970 (and were, therefore, 39 or older in 2008) were conservative versus 34 percent of those born in 1970 or later (and thus 38 or younger), and the situation in 2012 was little different.[3] This relatively small difference is certainly important, but probably not of huge significance for change, especially if one posits that the average person is likely to grow at least somewhat more conservative with age. Another way to view this is that there may be a drift toward greater conservatism with age, but that drift is evidently relatively mild because there are lots of younger conservatives to begin with.

In short, there are some demographic differences related to conservatism, particularly if one focuses on marital status, but age and gender are not crucial. The fact that marital status does matter is a bit of a tipoff. (And remember that these data are from a period prior to the rapid spread of gay marriage.) That traditional marriage and conservatism tend to go together suggests the obvious: traditional social beliefs of many sorts and conservatism also ought to go together. And indeed they do.

Race and Ethnicity

As noted in Chapter 2, at least since the early 1970s, Americans have been more likely to describe themselves as conservatives of some sort than as liberals, and since 1976 more likely to call themselves conservatives than either liberals or moderates. National surveys do not usually contain enough people for fine distinctions about ethnicity and, with the exception of Hispanics and African Americans, the number of respondents from other racial or ethnic groups (and bear in mind that race and ethnicity are slippery categories for designations that are primarily social in nature[4]) are usually too small for reliable analysis. Nevertheless, the data do contain some interesting suggestions about various groups or categories. Broadly speaking, whites may be the most conservative group, but Native American respondents (a tiny fraction of each sample) actually have a higher conservative score in several years. Asians have a very split pattern, although liberals outnumber conservatives in several years. For Hispanics, liberals outnumber conservatives in a little under half of the years, although there are also a few years where Hispanics score highest on conservatism, a topic I'll return to in the conclusion. Finally, African Americans stand out as the only racial group or category that consistently has more respondents scoring liberal than conservative. As noted previously, African Americans also vote so overwhelmingly for one party (the Democrats) that the ideology measure cannot be used to predict voting behavior.

Religion and Conservatism

One of the most potent factors associated with whether or not a person identifies as a conservative is religiosity. People who attend religious services regularly, say religion is important in their lives, and take the Bible literally are particularly likely to call themselves conservatives. One possible interpretation of these facts is that the relationship is caused by a kind of confusion. People who are "religious conservatives" or favor a conservative approach to "child rearing and family life" may be confused by what the term means in politics.[5] They may favor public policies in the economic realm that many would think of as liberal or tend to vote for more liberal candidates for office, for example, but their religious beliefs or traditional approaches to social life are the dominant factors that determine their reactions to the term conservative.[6] In short, the political content of much popular conservatism may be more a religious than a political affirmation. We'll come back to this after looking in more detail at the relationships themselves.

Table 3.1 Correlations (Gamma) between Attendance at Religious Services and Ideology, 1972–2012

Year	Correlation (Gamma*)
1972	−.19
1974	−.22
1976	−.24
1978	−.19
1980	−.18
1982	−.27
1984	−.19
1986	−.27
1988	−.21
1990**	−.20
1992	−.30
1994	−.28
1996	−.34
1998	−.30
2000	−.28
2002	−.33
2004	−.28
2008	−.33
2012	−.30

Data Source: 1972–2012 ANES

Note: African American respondents filtered out.

*Entries are the correlation (Gamma) coefficients between religious services and the Ideology measure.

**Question wording changed in 1990 from <u>Would you say you go to (church/synagogue) every week, almost every week, once or twice a month, a few times a year, or never?</u> to <u>Do you go to religious services every week, almost every week, once or twice a month, a few times a year, or never?</u>. However, the upward tick in the size of the relationship started in 1992, that is, the survey year after the wording change.

Question wording:
Ideology measure: Where would you place YOURSELF on this scale, or haven't you thought much about this? Extremely Liberal; Liberal; Slightly Liberal; Moderate; Middle of the Road; Slightly Conservative; Conservative; Extremely Conservative.

Religious service attendance: Do you go to religious services [EVERY WEEK, ALMOST EVERY WEEK, ONCE OR TWICE A MONTH, A FEW TIMES A YEAR, or NEVER]?

Starting with attendance at religious services, we have data for this that go back to 1972 (the first time ANES asked the ideology self-identification measure we are using). Relationships between conservatism and religious service attendance were moderately strong from 1972 to 1990 and then increased starting with the 1992 survey[7] (see Table 3.1). Nineteen ninety-two is also the year when those saying that they never attended religious services or had no religious preference began to rise. The average number of respondents who fell into the latter categories averaged about 21.5 percent over this 20-year period.[8] From 1992 to 2012, however, the average rose to 35 percent in the no preference or never categories. What basically happened is that not only has there been a noticeable falling off in the amount of religious service attendance reported over this period, but those who do attend services regularly are now more often conservative than they were previously. For example, in 1972, 47.7 percent of those who reported attending services every week self-identified as conservative. By 2008 and 2012 this percentage had risen to over 65 percent in each year (68.6 in 2008 and 65.7 in 2012).

When it comes to the importance of religion in people's lives, we see a similar pattern, although the time span of the available data is more limited. A simple question was asked, though not in all years, starting in 1980: "Do you consider religion to be an important part of your life, or not?" The relationship between the answers to this question and people's

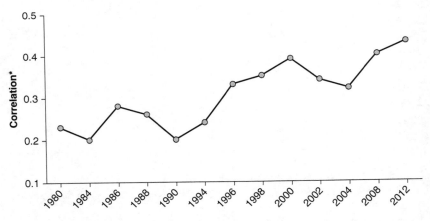

Figure 3.1 Ideology and the Importance of Religion in People's Lives, 1980–2012

Data Source: 1980–2012 ANES

Note: African American respondents filtered out.

*Entries are the correlation (Gamma) coefficients between the ideology measure and the importance of religion in people's lives measure.

Question wording:
Ideology measure: See Table 3.1.

Importance of religion: Do you consider religion to be an IMPORTANT part of your life, or NOT?

self-placement on the conservatism scale was moderately strong from 1980 through to 1994, and then much stronger starting in 1996 (averaging .23 for these years on the gamma measure of correlation and .37 for the years from 1996 to 2008). The strongest relationships were in 2008 and 2012. In addition, the overall percentage of respondents saying religion was important to them dropped from 71 percent in 1980 to 62 percent in 2008 and 65 percent in 2012, so while as a trend within the population the reported import of religion in people's lives was trending downward, the significance of religion as a predictor of conservatism was rising (see Figure 3.1).

Finally, starting in 1990, ANES asked people to answer a question about the Bible, with the options on a three-point scale ranging from "The Bible is the actual Word of God and is to be taken literally, word for word" to "The Bible is a book written by men and is not the word of God." (The middle option was: "the Bible is the Word of Got but not everything in it should be taken literally, word for word.") Again we see a modest, but noticeable increase in the strength of the relationship between this question and the ideology measure (53 percent of those who took the Bible literally identified as conservatives in 1990 versus 61 percent of similar believers in 2008), and a slight drop-off in the percentage of respondents believing that the Bible is the actual word of God (from 37 percent to 31 percent).[9]

The main point is that there are two trends running at once: a stronger relationship over time between various indicators of religiosity and self-identification as a conservative and, simultaneously, a consistent, although modest, fall-off in the percentage of people who are religious. Just to illustrate the strength of the relationship, in 2012 only 1 percent of respondents who described themselves as "Extremely Liberal" believed that the Bible is the literal word of God compared to 59 percent of those who chose the "Extremely Conservative" option who believed this.

So, in light of what's just been said, just how important is conservatism in determining political behavior? Perhaps it is true that many people who say they are conservative simply do so because they think that the term indicates that they are religious and, as a result, once one knows that they are religious there is little impact of their level of conservatism for their political choices

The initial test I propose is simple: Does the answer a respondent gives to the question about ideology (liberalism/conservatism) have any impact on vote choice once one takes into account how religious they are? Let's simply take a look at the impact that choices on the conservatism scale have on the voting choices within categories of religiosity (in social science jargon – with religiosity controlled). If one believes that respondents are simply conflating religious beliefs and conservatism, then there should be no relationship – just a lot of random noise – within categories of religiosity when one looks at the relationship between conservatism and vote choice, because religiosity alone should account for the choice.

In other words, whatever variation there is in the relationship between conservatism and vote choice within categories of religiosity should not be meaningful – it should just represent measurement error or some other type of meaningless choice made by people confronted by an array of options on a survey instrument.

But this is far from the case. The situation is much more complex. First, using the 2008 election data as the test, it is true that those who believe that the Bible is the literal word of God were much more likely to vote for John McCain, the more conservative of the two candidates, than for Barack Obama (77 percent to 23 percent). At the other end of the religiosity spectrum, among those who saw the Bible as written by men and not the word of God, the vote for Obama was 76 percent and for McCain, 24 percent. Those in the middle (viewing the Bible as the Word of God, but not literally so) were almost evenly split, with 47 percent for Obama and 53 percent for McCain. However, second, there is a strong relationship between the conservatism measure and vote choice within each category. The relatively few liberal respondents who take the Bible literally were much more likely to report voting for Obama than the more numerous conservatives in this group, and among those who thought that the Bible was written by men one finds the same relationship, with the more numerous liberals going strongly for Obama and the conservatives in the McCain camp. (For those who like correlation coefficients, the average gamma statistic is .80.)

The same pattern held in the 2012 data. While Romney was strongly favored by those who saw the Bible as the literal word of God (73 percent to 27 percent for Obama), he was supported by only 25 percent of those who believe the Bible was a book written by men and not the word of God. However, within the categories of the measure, the average correlation between ideology and vote was .85.

And the same basic pattern works for the two other indicators of religiosity I analyzed. When it comes to the importance of religion in people's lives, those who say it is important voted over 60 percent Republican in 2008 and 2012, while about 60 percent of those who said it was not important voted two to one for Obama, the Democratic candidate. As with the Bible question, the conservatism measure continued to hold within categories of the measure, with an average gamma coefficient of .84 in 2008 and .86 in 2012. Put in everyday terms, this reflects the fact that well over 90 percent of the self-identified liberals who said that religion was not important to them said they voted for Obama in the two election years, as contrasted to about 20 percent who voted for Obama of those for whom religion is not important but who identify as conservatives.

Turning to attendance at religious services, the findings are amazingly consistent, with 62 percent of respondents who attend religious services voting for McCain in 2008 and a like figure for Romney in 2012, contrasted to 41 percent who reported that they do not attend services

Table 3.2 Conservatives and Liberals Differ in Their Views on Social Issues, 2008 and 2012

*Conservative Are More Likely to:**	*2008*	*2012*
Want to limit abortion	−.43	−.42
Show less tolerance of people who live according to their own moral standards	−.36	−.32
Favor the death penalty for those convicted of murder	.39	.44
Oppose gay marriage	.55	.56
Oppose preferential hiring and promotion of blacks	.60	.41
Disagree that blacks have gotten less than they deserve	.32	.35
Believe that blacks must try harder to get ahead	−.30	−.30

Data Source: 2008 and 2012 ANES
Note: African Americans respondents filtered out.

*Entries are the correlations (Gamma) between the Ideology measure and the items listed below. Signs of correlations vary according to direction of item answer options.

<u>Question wordings:</u>
Ideology measure: See Table 3.1.

Want to limit abortion: There has been some discussion about abortion during recent years. Which one of the opinions on this page best agrees with your view? You can just tell me the number of the opinion you choose.

1 By law, abortion should never be permitted.
2 The law should permit abortion only in case of rape, incest, or when the woman's life is in danger.
3 The law should permit abortion for reasons other than rape, incest, or danger to the woman.
4 By law, a woman should always be able to obtain an abortion as a matter of personal choice.

Show less tolerance of people who live according to their own moral standard:
'We should be more tolerant of people who choose to live according to their own moral standards, even if they are very different from our own.' (Do you [AGREE STRONGLY, AGREE SOMEWHAT, NEITHER AGREE NOR DISAGREE, DISAGREE SOMEWHAT, or DISAGREE STRONGLY] with this statement?)

Favor the death penalty for those convicted of murder: Do you FAVOR or OPPOSE the death penalty for persons convicted of murder?

Oppose gay marriage: Which comes closest to your view? You can just tell me the number of your choice.

1 Gay and lesbian couples should be allowed to legally marry.
2 Gay and lesbian couples should be allowed to form civil unions but not legally marry.
3 There should be no legal recognition of a gay or lesbian couple's relationship.
4 Don't know.

Oppose preferential hiring and promotion of blacks: What about your opinion — are you FOR or AGAINST preferential hiring and promotion of blacks?

Disagree that blacks have gotten less than they deserve: 'Over the past few years, blacks have gotten less than they deserve.' (Do you [AGREE STRONGLY, AGREE

(continued)

Table 3.1 (continued)

SOMEWHAT, NEITHER AGREE NOR DISAGREE, DISAGREE SOMEWHAT, or DISAGREE STRONGLY] with this statement?)

Believe that blacks must try harder to get ahead: 'It's really a matter of some people not trying hard enough; if blacks would only try harder they could be just as well off as whites.' (Do you [AGREE STRONGLY, AGREE SOMEWHAT, NEITHER AGREE NOR DISAGREE, DISAGREE SOMEWHAT, or DISAGREE STRONGLY] with this statement?)

aside from the occasional wedding, baptism, or funeral voting for the Republican in each year. And within each category of church attendance or non-attendance, there was the familiar and strong relationship between choices on the conservatism measure and vote choice (average gamma equal to .84 in 2008 and .87 in 2012).

In short, based on these findings, religious people are more likely to say they are conservative and for some that's probably the whole story. But for many others, it is more than that. Notions about conservatism and liberalism are strong enough that they drive vote choice in a quite meaningful way, even showing a definite impact when there is a conflict between the normal choices of those who are religious and a respondent's position on the ideology scale. The inference I draw is that the term conservative is not just a synonym for religious, though religious people definitely tend to be more conservative. Clearly, expressed conservatism for many in the population seems to be more than simply an affirmation of their religiosity.

Social Beliefs and Conservatism

Given what we know about religion and conservatism, it is no surprise that similar divides exist on many of the social issues that mark American politics. Table 3.2 presents relationships between measures of some of these variables and ideology.[10] To summarize: Those who call themselves conservatives are most likely to want restrictions on abortion (or its abolition as a legal choice). The same relationship with conservatism is present for those who have low tolerance for non-traditional moral standards. It is also the case with those who favor the use of the death penalty. Similarly, conservatives tend to be the members of society who are most likely to oppose gay marriage and they are also the segment of the population most likely to oppose things like affirmative action in the hiring and promotion of African Americans, to believe that blacks must try harder to get ahead, and to disagree that blacks have gotten less than they deserve.

Starting with abortion and, for the moment, limiting ourselves to the 2008 and 2012 data, the relationship between conservatism and views on abortion is strong and clear. Less than 8 percent of those who describe themselves as extremely liberal say abortion should never be legal compared to well over a third of those who describe themselves as extremely conservative. Looked at from the other side of the coin, on abortion permissiveness a full 72 percent of extreme liberals in 2008 (but also 73 percent of those who just called themselves liberal without the extreme modifier) said abortion should always be legal. The figures for 2012 are 82 percent and 76 percent respectively. That compares to fewer than 23 percent of conservatives or "extreme" conservatives who said the same thing in either year. As we shall see in Chapter 5, this strong relationship was not always the case, but it quite clearly exists now and it has roiled American politics for a good number of years.

When it comes to tolerance of those with different moral standards, liberals profess great tolerance and conservatives, while certainly not all intolerant, are much less tolerant. In answer to a question that asked people whether they "should be more tolerant of people who choose to live according to their own moral standards, even if they are very different from our own," 67 percent of "Extremely Liberal" respondents agreed strongly and another 18 percent agreed somewhat in 2008, and a combined total of 83 percent agreed in 2012. Among those who simply called themselves liberals, the figures were 48 percent and 40 percent respectively for the two categories of agreement in 2008 and 41 and 46 percent in 2012. In short, well over 80 percent of liberals expressed tolerance of those with different moral standards. The figures are quite different for conservatives, where the percentages that agree strongly or agree that they should be more tolerant of those who live according to their own moral standards falls dramatically. Over 40 percent of conservatives, in fact, were on the other end of the spectrum in 2008, expressing disagreement that they should be more tolerant of those who live by different moral standards and about the same percentage expressed similar views in 2012. Assuming that they do not start from an assumption that they are already quite tolerant of others with different moral standards, the relationship is very strong indeed.

Turning next to the death penalty for persons convicted of murder, conservatives overwhelmingly favor the death penalty – an average over 80 percent of people who describe themselves as either extremely conservative or just plain conservative in 2008 and 2012 and even about 75 percent of those who identified as slightly conservative (Table 3.3). That puts them close to the population as a whole, where just over 70 percent favor the death penalty for murder. That figure drops below 70 percent for those who were slightly liberal in 2008 and 2012 and stood at about 50 percent for those who chose the simple liberal label. It is only among "Extremely Liberal" types that the percentage favoring the death penalty drops below 50 percent (to a little less than a third – 32 percent in 2008 and 40 percent in 2012). In short, one knows a lot about just how likely a person is to favor the death penalty by whether he or she is a conservative, but it is important to understand that here the conservative issue position predominates, with only a majority of "Extremely Liberal" people (who are a small percentage of the total population sample) taking a position opposed to the death penalty.[11]

Table 3.3 Percent in Favor of Death Penalty, by Ideology, 2008 and 2012

Ideology	Percentage in Favor of Death Penalty	
	2008	2012
Extremely Liberal	32.3	40.0
Liberal	50.4	55.0
Slightly Liberal	65.7	68.0
Moderate	76.8	79.7
Slightly Conservative	74.4	77.0
Conservative	82.4	86.0
Extremely Conservative	86.3	77.6
Overall Percent	72.0	75.4
Gamma	−.36	−.32

Data source: 2008 and 2012 ANES
Note: African American Respondents filtered out.

Question wording:.
Death penalty: See Table 3.2 note.
Ideology measure: See Figure 3.1 note.

As in many other areas, by the way, one can't predict how African Americans regard the death penalty by whether or not they identify conservative or liberal. However, it is worth noting that even among African Americans almost 45 percent of respondents expressed approval of the death penalty in 2008 and 56 percent did so in 2012, and this in a nation where African Americans are the disproportionate recipients of this ultimate penalty.

I will leave a fuller treatment of the implications of views on gays to the concluding chapter, but needless to say conservatives hold more conservative views on issues connected to homosexuality than liberals. On the gay marriage issue (this prior to later court decisions), the relationship between ideology and approval of gay marriage is strong and consistent. In 2008, for example, liberals of all stripes believed that gay marriage should be allowed, while among those identifying as "Conservative" or "Extremely Conservative" respondents were opposed. ("Slightly Conservative" respondents were more moderate in their opposition, tending to favor civil unions, though not marriage.) The figures look quite similar in 2012, though in this year support for civil unions grew noticeably among conservatives, while liberals' support for the rights of gays to marry remained steadfast.[12]

Finally, let's look at views about how American society should deal with the legacy of discrimination (and worse) against African Americans.

The issue I will focus on here is preferential hiring and promotion of blacks as a partial way to redress past injustices.

What the data in Table 3.4 show is a very strong relationship between self-placement on the liberalism/conservatism scale and views on preferential hiring and promotion, although again the relationship is set against an overall view that is prominent in the society, only here there is overwhelming opposition among non-blacks to preferential hiring and promotion for blacks – almost 90 percent of the non-black respondents opposed preferential hiring in 2008 and 2012 (and even about 40 percent of blacks were opposed in each year). Opposition among all types of conservatives was an average 94 percent in the two years. It was 91 percent for moderates in 2008 and 84 percent in 2012, and in the 75 percent and above range for those who described themselves as "Liberal" or "Slightly Liberal." Only "Extremely Liberal" self-identifiers supported preferential hiring and promotion and even here the percentage barely topped 50 in 2008 and was 47 percent in 2012. In short, conservatives are quite a bit more likely than liberals to oppose preferential hiring and promotion, but it is also the case that there is a more general societal tendency in that direction (i.e. opposition). I should note that not all civil rights attitudes show such lopsided percentages against, but in each case if one takes the average societal result (for or against) as a base, conservatives tend to be more to one side of the issue as stated in the question (the conventionally

Table 3.4 Percent Opposing Preferential Hiring of Blacks, by Ideology, 2008 and 2012

Ideology	Percentage Opposing Preferential Hiring of Blacks	
	2008	*2012*
Extremely Liberal	48.5	53.2
Liberal	74.1	74.4
Slightly Liberal	86.9	82.9
Moderate	90.8	86.2
Slightly Conservative	95.4	91.1
Conservative	97.3	94.3
Extremely Conservative	96.8	92.1
Overall Percent	89.5	86.5
Gamma	.60	.41

Data source: 2008 and 2012 ANES

Note: African American Respondents filtered out.

Question wording:.

Preferential hiring: See Table 3.2 note.

Ideology measure: See Figure 3.1 note.

conservative side at the time, in keeping with other findings discussed so far) and liberals tend to be more on the other side.

I'll close with two examples of both societal perspectives on questions related to race and the relationship of conservatism to these perspectives. When respondents were asked how strongly they disagreed with a statement that blacks have gotten less than they deserve, the overall reaction of the non-African American part of the population is to disagree, that is to say that this is not so (55 percent in 2008, and 62 percent in 2012), and about a quarter of the respondents in the middle (neither agreeing nor disagreeing). And, these distributions are related to the degree of conservatism expressed. For example, in 2012 about 80 percent of "Extremely Conservative" respondents disagreed either somewhat or strongly with the statement, as did a similar percentage of those who simply labeled themselves as conservative (unmodified). Similarly, when it came to a statement that "blacks must try harder to get ahead," 58 percent of respondents (recall that these results do not include black respondents) agreed in 2008 and 53 percent did the same in 2012. Again, those anchoring the conservative end of the scale were most likely to take what might generously be termed the skeptical position about blacks, with the combined proportion of "Conservative" and "Extremely Conservative" respondents who took the position that blacks need to try harder averaging at about 70 percent (as opposed to between 20 and 33 percent in the top tier liberal categories – "Extremely Liberal" and "Liberal").

Conclusion

Of the many demographic categories considered in this chapter (region, gender, age, and marital status), marital status stands out. Married people are significantly more conservative than people who are unmarried. Indeed, various traditional lifestyle indicators and social beliefs are important factors in understanding which people are likely to identify as conservatives. Those people who attend religious services regularly, who say that religion is important in their lives and who take the bible literally are particularly likely to call themselves conservatives. The data also indicate two simultaneous trends: 1. a stronger relationship over time between various indicators of religiosity and self-identification as a conservative; and 2. simultaneously, a consistent, although modest, fall-off in the percentage of people who are religious. In addition, the data suggest that while religious people definitely tend to be more conservative, expressed conservatism is more than simply an affirmation of religiosity. Even within categories of religiosity, where one places oneself on a measure of conservatism/liberalism matters for such things as vote choice. It appears to be simply untrue that religious conservatives (or others in the general public who identify as conservatives, for that matter) can be dismissed as simply confused by what the term conservative means in politics.

Conservatives are less tolerant of those with different (i.e. unconventional) moral standards. They are more likely than liberals to favor the death penalty for murder. And, in this post-1960s civil rights legislation era, they are less likely than liberals to favor such policies as preferential hiring and promotion for blacks or to believe that generations of slavery and discrimination have made it more difficult for blacks to work their way up.

In short, and consistent with the widespread image of them, conservatives tend to be conventional people with – well, let's put it simply – conventionally conservative (that is, traditional, complete with the baggage that term implies) views on social issues. The next question is whether they are also conservative on economic issues and on issues connected to the role of government in society.

Endnotes

1 The figures for 2010 show higher levels of conservatism all around due, most likely to the question wording – no option for say "don't know" or "haven't thought about it," but the overall regional difference is about 15 points, 63 percent conservative in the South and 48 percent conservative in the North.
2 Forty seven percent of the married identified as conservative in 2012 versus 32 percent of the never married and 37 percent of those who were divorced.
3 Thirty-five percent of younger people (up to 39) were self-identified conservatives in 2012 versus 46 percent of those 40 and over. (African Americans, as is the case in the analyses, unless otherwise noted, were not included in these calculations.)
4 I have been including the "Other" category in the analyses when filtering out African Americans. I later learned that ANES had reassigned some of these respondents in 2008 to substantive categories, including the African American category. I did not then do the same for two reasons: 1) Any respondent who was in the Other category initially, based on his or her answer to the racial or ethnic group question (v0831251a) probably had a highly complex identity to begin with; and 2) Tests indicated that re-classifying respondents would make no significant difference in the numerous results already completed and written up.
5 Christopher Ellis and James A. Stimson, *Ideology in America* (New York: Cambridge University Press, 2012), page 133.
6 Ellis and Stimson *Ideology in America* (2012), page 144.
7 The average correlation (gamma) between the two was .19 for the years from 1972 to 1990. The average from 1992 to 2008 was .27. The Moral Majority was founded in 1979; it was followed by the Christian Coalition in 1989. William Martin stresses that their influence grew gradually from initial concerns about the impact of liberalism on the nation's family and moral base to concerns about government tax exemptions for de facto segregated Christian academies. By 1992, however, their influence became especially clear. See William Martin, *With God on Our Side: The Rise of the Religious Right in America* (New York: Broadway Books, 2005), especially pages 173 and 326.

8 There was a slight question wording change in 1990 in the item measuring religions service attendance, but that is clearly not the cause of the uptick in non-attendance since it began in 1992.

9 The gamma coefficient between the two variables was –.35 in 1990 and an average of –.42 in 2008 and 2012.

10 The discussions here are sometimes relatively brief because I will take up some of these issues again in Chapter 5 and in the concluding chapter (9).

11 See Frank R. Baumgartner, Suzanna L. De Boef and Amber E. Boydstun, *The Decline of the Death Penalty and the Discovery of Innocence* (New York: Cambridge University Press, 2008), page 5, who argue, using Gallup data, that support for capital punishment, while high, has been dropping. They say (page 5): "Although Americans remain supportive of capital punishment *in theory*, they are increasingly concerned that the system might not work as intended *in practice*."

12 I'll look at the long-term changes that took place in support for gays in the military in the conclusion, but an idea to keep in mind is that while liberals and conservatives may differ strongly on issues such as gay marriage or gays in the military or other contentious matters at any point in time, these differences do not necessarily preclude changes in overall societal views on the issue over the long term.

4   The Size and Role of Government

This chapter examines the beliefs of conservatives about issues connected to the size and role of government in society. At first blush, this should be a very straight-forward task. A stereotype of American conservatives is that they are convinced free-marketeers who support the most limited role possible for government, especially in areas connected to the economy. That may well be true of some, but, as we shall see, the situation is more complicated. The rhetoric of the free market and related beliefs about the size and role of government and the realities of life do not always rest comfortably together, even for people who call themselves conservatives and, I should emphasize, traditional conservatism did not always bless free markets (certainly not unequivocally). Indeed, the relationship of conservatism to economic issues is one of complexity and change.

What the data will show is that in what might be called purely ideological terms, people who call themselves conservatives have clear and consistent views on broadly stated issues connected to the size and role of government (and on program proposals for expanding the role of government). They want a smaller and less intrusive government. But there can be a disjunction between beliefs that focus on principles and those that focus on spending in practice. So we might find that the same people who are clear and consistent when they are asked to identify themselves ideologically (on a scale from conservative to liberal) and to specify their beliefs about the role of the government in the economy are not necessarily going to say consistent things about the actual benefits that come from government programs. This presents the leaders of American conservatism, especially those in elective office, with a sometimes uncomfortable dilemma; just how far to go in implementing the market-oriented dogma that is an element of much of contemporary American conservatism.

Finally, there are also signs that conservatives in the general public are willing to accept the idea – at least more than moderates and liberals do – that spending on established government programs should be contained or even decreased. That is still far from the crucial test – reactions to actual cuts – but it does suggest at least a bit of a retreat from a public that has been characterized by prominent analysts as philosophically conservative and operationally liberal, that is "committed to minimal government and maximum liberty for individuals to pursue their interests," but also "devoted to specific and concrete government programs."[1]

Philosophical Conservatives

When it comes to beliefs about the size and role of government, conservatives in the general public (as well as much of the conservative elite) differ considerably from liberals. They are much more likely to say that less government is better, that government has gotten inappropriately bigger because it is involved in things that people should handle for themselves, that there should be less spending on services, that the free market is a better mechanism than the government for handling the complex economic problems the country faces today, that private health insurance plans are a better way to handle health care than government-provided health insurance plans, and that the government should not guarantee either jobs or individuals' standard of living. Their ideal world is market-driven, with individuals taking major responsibility for themselves and their families. For them, the notion expressed by Hillary Clinton in the title of a book published in 1996 that "it takes a village" (in this case, to raise a child) would be anathema.[2] What it takes are responsible individuals. Or, in a famous quote from Margaret Thatcher: "And, you know, there's no such thing as society. There are individual men and women and there are families. And no government can do anything except through people, and people must look after themselves first. It is our duty to look after ourselves and then, also, to look after our neighbours."[3]

A look at Table 4.1 will provide clear confirmation of the strong relationship between a respondent's expressed conservatism and views about the size and role of government. The table shows the gamma correlations in 2008 and 2012 between the conservatism measure and a variety of measures indicating how people feel about what the role of government should be, *at least in principle*. (One measure covers health insurance, but the Affordable Care Act had yet to be passed in 2008 or significantly implemented in 2012.) All of the relationships are strong and in the predicted direction (depending on the wording of the question). They also show a pattern that we will see again in a later section of the chapter, namely that the coefficients are slightly stronger in 2012 than in 2008.

Let's examine a few examples.

Respondents were asked a relatively simple question about the role of government with two options as answers: "the less government the better" and "more things government should be doing." That indicator was strongly related to conservatism in both 2008 and 2012, but there is also evidence of change towards an even stronger relationship in 2012 and an increase in the percentage of people choosing "the less government the better" option (Table 4.2a).

Table 4.1 Conservatives and Liberals Differ in Their Views on the Size and Role of Government (and on Proposed Social Service or Benefit Programs), 2008 and 2012*

Conservatives More Likely To:	2008	2012
Believe less government is better	−.45	−.55
Believe government is bigger because it is involved in things people should handle themselves	−.50	−.59
Want less government spending on services	−.45	−.53
Favor the free market to handle today's complex economic problems	.47	.59
Oppose government provided health insurance plans and favor private plans	.39	.58
Favor jobs over protecting the environment	.36	.53

Data source: 2008 and 2012 ANES

Note: African American Respondents filtered out.

*Entries are Gamma coefficients of the relationship between the Ideology measure and the items listed below:

Question wordings:

Ideology measure: Where would you place YOURSELF on this scale, or haven't you thought much about this? Extremely Liberal; Liberal; Slightly Liberal; Moderate; Middle of the Road; Slightly Conservative; Conservative; Extremely Conservative.

More or less government: I am going to ask you to choose which of two statements I read comes closer to your own opinion. You might agree to some extent with both, but we want to know which one is closer to your own views.
ONE, the less government, the better; OR
TWO, there are more things that government should be doing?
{IF NECESSARY, PROBE "WHICH IS CLOSER"}

Government size: I am going to ask you to choose which of two statements I read comes closer to your own opinion. You might agree to some extent with both, but we want to know which one is closer to your own views. ONE, the main reason government has become bigger over the years is because it has gotten involved in things that people should do for themselves; OR
TWO, government has become bigger because the problems we face have become bigger.
{IF NECESSARY, PROBE "WHICH IS CLOSER"}

Government spending on services: Some people think the government should provide fewer services even in areas such as health and education in order to reduce spending. Suppose these people are at one end of a scale, at point 1. Other people feel it is important for the government to provide many more services even if it means an increase in spending. Suppose these people are at the other end, at point 7. And, of course, some other people have opinions somewhere in between, at points 2, 3, 4, 5 or 6.
Where would you place YOURSELF on this scale, or haven't you thought much about this?
1. Govt should provide many fewer services,
. . .
7. Govt should provide many more services.

Government and economic problems: I am going to ask you to choose which of two statements I read comes closer to your own opinion. You might agree to some extent with both, but we want to know which one is closer to your own views.

(continued)

Table 4.1 (continued)

ONE, we need a strong government to handle today's complex economic problems; OR TWO, the free market can handle these problems without government being involved. {IF NECESSARY, PROBE "WHICH IS CLOSER"}

Government or private health insurance: There is much concern about the rapid rise in medical and hospital costs. Some people feel there should be a government insurance plan which would cover all medical and hospital expenses for everyone. Suppose these people are at one end of a scale, at point 1. Others feel that all medical expenses should be paid by individuals through private insurance plans like Blue Cross or other company paid plans. Suppose these people are at the other end, at point 7. And, of course, some other people have opinions somewhere in between, at points 2, 3, 4, 5, or 6.

Where would you place YOURSELF on this scale, or haven't you thought much about this?

1. Govt insurance plan,

. . .

7. Private insurance plan.

Government and the environment: Some people think it is important to protect the environment even if it costs some jobs or otherwise reduces our standard of living. (Suppose these people are at one end of the scale, at point number 1). Other people think that protecting the environment is not as important as maintaining jobs or our standard of living.

(Suppose these people are at the other end of the scale, at point number 7. And of course, some other people have opinions somewhere in between, at points 2, 3, 4, 5, or 6).

Where would you place YOURSELF on this scale, or haven't you thought much about this?

1. Protect environment, even if it costs jobs & standard of living,

. . .

7. Jobs & standard of living more important than environment.

Table 4.2a Percent Saying "The Less Government the Better," by Ideology, 2008 and 2012

Ideology	Percent Saying: "The Less Government the Better"	
	2008	2012
Extremely Liberal	25.2	20.1
Liberal	23.6	29.7
Slightly Liberal	44.3	43.4
Moderate	36.3	53.7
Slightly Conservative	59.6	75.5
Conservative	71.7	84.0
Extremely Conservative	72.1	82.1
Overall Percent	49.4	60.4
Gamma	−.45	−.55

Data source: 2008 and 2012 ANES
Note: African American Respondents filtered out.

Question wording:
Ideology measure: See Table 4.1 note.

Government size: ONE, the less government, the better; OR TWO, there are more things that government should be doing?

The table shows that the percentage of people saying "the less government the better" increased from a little under 50 percent in 2008 to 60 percent in 2012. In addition, the gamma coefficient for the relationship between answers to this question and the ideology measure increased from −.45 to −.55. The reason for the latter can be seen in the increase in "the less government the better" views among people in the "Conservative" and "Extremely Conservative" categories, where the percentage saying "the less government the better" went from the low 70s to the mid-80s.

Table 4.2b shows the relationship between a respondent's answers to a simple question about why the government has gotten bigger, a question strongly related to the "less government the better" item used in Table 4.2a.[4] One option for answering the question was that "the main reason that the government has gotten bigger over the years is because it has gotten involved in things that people should do for themselves." The other was that "government has become bigger because the problems we face have become bigger." The first thing to say here is that half the people or more in each year chose the option that government has gotten bigger because it has gotten involved in

Table 4.2b Percent Saying "Government Is Bigger Because It's Involved in Things People Should Do for Themselves," by Ideology, 2008 and 2012

Ideology	Percent Saying: "Government is bigger because it's involved in things people should do for themselves."	
	2008	2012
Extremely Liberal	19.2	13.5
Liberal	22.9	28.2
Slightly Liberal	42.1	39.0
Moderate	38.1	56.3
Slightly Conservative	61.3	72.0
Conservative	74.8	87.0
Extremely Conservative	79.6	84.8
Overall Percent	51.0	61.0
Gamma	−.50	−.59

Data source: 2008 and 2012 ANES
Note: African American Respondents filtered out.
Question wording:
Ideology measure: See Table 4.1.

Government is bigger: ONE, the main reason government has become bigger over the years is because it has gotten involved in things that people should do for themselves; OR: TWO, government has become bigger because the problems we face have become bigger.

doing things people should be doing for themselves. (About 51 percent answered this way in 2008 and 61 percent in 2012, an increase of about 10 percent in the conventionally conservative answer, mirroring the finding in Table 4.2a where the percentage increase in those saying "the less government the better" was also about 10 percent.)

The spread in answers across categories of the ideology measure is considerable. In 2012, just to take the last year for which we have data, almost 85 percent of people who classified themselves as "Extremely Conservative" or "Conservative" (unmodified) said that the government is bigger because it is doing things that people should be doing for themselves. On the other end of the spectrum, less than 14 percent of "Extremely Liberal" people chose this option and 28 percent of those who were "Liberal" (unmodified) did the same. In other words, most liberals and conservatives gave completely different reasons for government growth, reasons that align perfectly with their overall classification of themselves as liberals or conservatives.

The same pattern exists for all of the relationships in Table 4.1. In each case, the gamma coefficient is higher in 2012 than in 2008 and the percentage of respondents giving the more conservative answer to the survey question has increased also. For example, the proportion of people wanting less government spending on services increased from 33 percent to 47 percent and the gamma coefficient went from −.43 to −.53. Again, as with the other indicators, the proportion of conservatives, particularly those who firmly identify as conservatives (those choosing the "Conservative" or "Extremely Conservative" labels for themselves), who endorse spending less on services rose from about 60 percent to 80 percent. Similar findings hold for favoring the free market over the government to handle complex economic problems and opposing government-provided health insurance plans – the view of about 70 percent of conservatives in 2008; rising to about 80 percent in 2012.

In brief, there is a consistent pattern of strong relationships between indicators of what I call here philosophical conservatism – views about the role of the market and about the role of government versus that of the individual – and whether or not someone identifies as a conservative. And not only is the relationship strong, but it appears to have grown stronger over the last few years. In other words, while the proportion of people calling themselves conservative has not changed much, the proportion of people in the public taking the more conservative position on the types of issues in Table 4.1 has increased a bit and the proportion of conservatives holding these views has also increased. The division in the US on these issues, in short, is growing more pronounced, with conservatives more and more likely to take a position against a government role.

Operational Liberals?

While the relationship between ideological self-identification and relatively abstract views about the role of the market and about the role of government versus that of the individual may be strong and getting stronger, the picture muddies when one deals with views about actual public programs and how much should be spent on them. Here one finds that conservatives are often, as the philosophical conservative/operational liberal hypothesis suggests, quite supportive of spending on programs and benefits. There are also, however, clear differences in these areas between conservatives and liberals in their level of support, especially for spending increases, and overall indications of a drop in support for increased federal spending.

A look at Table 4.3 is a beginning in illustrating these tendencies. The table examines the relationship between the ideology indicator and opinions on federal spending on domestic programs in both the 2008 and 2012 ANES election surveys. The opinions on spending cover a wide range of issues and the results suggest emerging change in some areas.

Table 4.3 Are Conservatives Operational Liberals? Correlations (Gamma) of Ideology and Views on Federal Spending, 2008 and 2012*

	2008	*2012*
Spending on Science and Technology	.10	.24
Spending on Social Security	.21	.17
Spending on Aid to Public Schools	.41	.24
Spending Dealing with Crime	−.11	.01
Spending on Welfare	.30	.46
Spending on the Environment	.45	.53
Spending on Aid to the Poor	.41	.40
Spending on Child Care	.45	.37

Data source: 2008 and 2012 ANES
Note: African American Respondents filtered out.

*Entries are Gamma coefficients of the relationship between the Ideology measure and the items listed in the table.

<u>Question Wordings</u>:
Ideology measure: See Table 4.1 note.

Federal programs/issues area: Should federal spending on [federal program/issue area] be INCREASED, DECREASED, or kept ABOUT THE SAME?
[Wordings of federal programs and issue areas are as stated in table.]

Note: All recoded to:
1 = Increased
2 = Kept the same
3 = Decreased; Cut out entirely.

If we examine the first column (relationships in 2008), we see that a majority of the gamma coefficients (five of the eight) are .30 or above. Liberals were more likely to favor increased or stable federal spending in these areas than conservatives, but the coefficients suggest that the differences between them were relatively moderate in some areas such as Social Security and science and technology and only very modestly negative when it comes to spending on crime (here conservatives are slightly more willing to increase spending). Overall, however, the coefficients in 2008 reflect differences between liberals and conservatives in many "operational" areas of government spending, including even modest differences on programs such as Social Security.

The coefficients for 2012 show movement in some areas, up somewhat, for example, when it comes to spending on science and technology and down on spending on public schools, but generally they are best characterized as stable. However, there is an interesting story beneath these coefficients that add to the story. I shall use a few examples to portray that story.

Table 4.4 looks at one of the best established and most popular social programs in the United States – Social Security. The gamma coefficients for the relationship between a respondent's self-described ideology and his or her views on spending on Social Security are, as noted, relatively moderate. Liberals are more likely to favor increased spending than conservatives, but even 51 percent of the "Extremely Conservative" favor increases, certainly in line with the "operational liberal" notion. However, while in 2012 the correlation between ideology and views on spending on Social Security is basically the same as in 2008, the overall percentage in favor of increased spending has fallen below 50 percent and now all listed categories of conservatives are at 40 percent or below in espousing this view. (Liberals are also less likely to favor increased spending in this area; hence the gamma statistic is just about the same in the two years.) Where the change came from is in the "keep the same" category. It was at about 32 percent in 2008 and rose to almost 50 percent in 2012. So while these data do not undermine the notion that the population may be reasonably described as "operationally liberal" on Social Security, they do show an overall movement away from the most stereotypically liberal position on the issue, that is, increased spending.

Table 4.5, showing more detail on the relationship between ideology and opinion on federal spending on aid to public schools, is a more dramatic example because both the coefficient and the endorsement of increased federal expenditures show a decrease. Where in 2008 almost all liberals (more than 80 percent averaging the three liberal categories) favored an increase in federal spending on public schools, conservatives (except for the most extreme) also endorsed more federal spending in this area. However, in 2012, overall endorsement of increased federal spending

Table 4.4 Percent Favoring an Increase in Federal Spending on Social Security, by Ideology, 2008 and 2012

Ideology	Percentage in Favor of an Increase	
	2008	2012
Extremely Liberal	71	55
Liberal	68	46
Slightly Liberal	65	46
Moderate	69	51
Slightly Conservative	63	40
Conservative	53	33
Extremely Conservative	51	38
Overall Percent	64	44
Gamma	.17	.17

Data source: 2008 and 2012 ANES
Note: African American respondents filtered out.
Question wording:
See Table 4.1 and Table 4.3 notes.

Table 4.5 Percent Favoring an Increase in Federal Spending on Aid to Public Schools, by Ideology, 2008 and 2012

Ideology	Percentage in Favor of an Increase	
	2008	2012
Extremely Liberal	91	69
Liberal	89	64
Slightly Liberal	80	57
Moderate	76	43
Slightly Conservative	71	46
Conservative	59	36
Extremely Conservative	46	32
Overall Percent	73	46
Gamma	.40	.24

Data source: 2008 and 2012 ANES
Note: African American respondents filtered out.
Question wording:
See Table 4.1 and Table 4.3 notes.

fell quite substantially and no category of conservative (and, indeed, not even moderates) supported increased federal spending. On the other hand, the tradeoff was between increased spending and spending remaining the same; in other words, few in either year supported decreased spending (5 percent in 2008 and 13 percent in 2012).

The next two tables (4.6 and 4.7) show areas where the gamma coefficients in the two years are strong and consistently high, but the underlying data reveal quite a bit of change. What's basically happened is that support for increased spending has dropped. Starting with Table 4.6, we can see in comparing 2008 and 2012 data that the bottom has fallen out among conservatives in terms of increased federal spending on aid to the poor, and such support has decreased among liberals as well, dropping beneath 50 percent for all but those who chose to describe themselves as "Extremely Liberal." Further, where fewer than 10 percent wanted to spend less on the poor in 2008, that percentage increased to 23 percent in 2012.

The data in Table 4.7 are very similar. Behind the modest increase in the gamma coefficient and the big drop in the overall percentage favoring increased federal spending on the environment is an almost complete collapse of support for increased spending between the two years among those in each sample who described themselves as "Conservative" or "Extremely Conservative" and a big drop among other conservatives and moderates as well. The percentages who wanted to decrease spending on environmental programs went from 7 percent in the 2008 data to 20

Table 4.6 Percent Favoring an Increase in Federal Spending on Aid to the Poor, by Ideology, 2008 and 2012

Ideology	Percentage in Favor of an Increase	
	2008	*2012*
Extremely Liberal	88	72
Liberal	98	47
Slightly Liberal	66	36
Moderate	66	36
Slightly Conservative	51	23
Conservative	44	13
Extremely Conservative	39	14
Overall Percent	60	30
Gamma	.37	.40

Data source: 2008 and 2012 ANES
Note: African American respondents filtered out.
Question wording:
See Table 4.1 and Table 4.3 notes.

Table 4.7 Percent Favoring an Increase in Federal Spending on the Environment, by Ideology, 2008 and 2012

Ideology	Percentage in Favor of an Increase	
	2008	2012
Extremely Liberal	93	86
Liberal	84	69
Slightly Liberal	76	53
Moderate	69	39
Slightly Conservative	64	31
Conservative	44	15
Extremely Conservative	36	13
Overall Percent	65	38
Gamma	.44	.53

Data source: 2008 and 2012 ANES
Note: African American respondents filtered out.

Question wording:
See Table 4.1 and Table 4.3 notes.

percent in 2012 (19.6 percent to be exact), but the only conservative group favoring a decrease in spending was the "Extremely Conservative."

It will come as little surprise that data on federal spending on welfare (Table 4.8) look different from the previous areas in one respect; in 2008 32 percent wanted to decrease spending in this area, and that percentage was up to a little over 50 percent in 2012. In tune with this, even for the "Extremely Liberal," support for increased spending fell below 50 percent in 2012, and the percent wanting a decrease was over 70 percent on average for conservatives (compared to less than 20 percent on average for conservatives of all types in 2008).

Support for federal spending in the other areas listed in Table 4.3 also fell, though by only about 10 percent when it comes to spending on science and technology or on crime, but by over 30 percent for spending on child care. In the latter case, however, while about a little over 40 percent of the most conservative favored a decrease in federal spending on child care in 2012, the percentages were far from those favoring a decrease in spending on welfare.

Conclusion

Conservatives and liberals in the general public are split on what we can call philosophical propositions about the size and role of government. People who identify as conservatives say that they want a smaller and

Table 4.8 Percent Favoring an Increase in Federal Spending on Welfare, by Ideology, 2008 and 2012

Ideology	Percentage in Favor of an Increase	
	2008	2012
Extremely Liberal	55.0	43.2
Liberal	43.6	21.9
Slightly Liberal	24.2	12.6
Moderate	23.0	12.2
Slightly Conservative	20.1	7.2
Conservative	14.9	2.7
Extremely Conservative	16.4	6.9
Overall Percent	24.5	11.1
Gamma	.30	.46

Data source: 2008 and 2012 ANES
Note: African American respondents filtered out.

Question wording:
See Table 4.1 and Table 4.3 notes.

more limited government, at least in theory, and people who call themselves liberals say that they want a larger and more active government. At the same time, there is a general tendency for many of those same people (of either persuasion) to want either more or at least the current level of federal expenditures in a variety of areas, including for purposes that one might identify as favored by liberals such as Social Security and aid to the poor. (The most glaring exception is welfare, an area with high racial overtones, even though more non-African Americans are welfare recipients than African Americans.[5]) There are also clear signs in the 2012 data of an overall drop in support for increased federal expenditures, one that affects liberals as well as conservatives. And it is clearly the case that in many areas conservatives are less likely than liberals to favor increased federal expenditures, and that this was the case in both 2008 and 2012.

So where does this leave us? First, certainly, in absolute terms, the "operational liberal" concept fits the public at large in most of the areas we have looked at in this chapter – the one major exception is welfare programs, and even here only 50 percent of all respondents in 2012 wanted to see a decrease in federal expenditures. However, there is clearly a split between liberals and conservatives in many of these areas, with liberals favoring increases in expenditures and a larger percentage of the more conservative endorsing the status quo. And, to repeat, in the most controversial areas like welfare and aid to the poor, there were quite significant percentages of conservatives who favored cuts in 2012. In essence, the self-identified conservative part of the public is, on average, more conservative on federal expenditures than the self-identified liberal or moderate part. That may not make them full "operational conservatives," but it does indicate a decided difference on federal expenditures in many areas between liberals and conservatives. And this conclusion is set in an atmosphere of an apparent overall decline in public support for increases in federal expenditures. Second, since it is the most conservative who are the most likely to favor cuts (and, as we shall see, to vote in primaries), the data suggest why Republican candidates and elected officials are the most willing to take positions on program expenditures that go beyond the clichés connected to general opposition to the size and role of government, though clearly they tread carefully in many of these areas. Finally, a cautionary note on the meaning of the findings: Even as the relationships between ideology and views on federal spending in various areas stand now, it is worth noting that one should be careful in interpreting what a conservative position ought to be on spending. For the most part, it is safe to say that conservatives traditionally are wary of great spending, especially on domestic programs, but traditional conservatives are also wary of upsetting the status quo. Therefore, that a majority of conservatives in national surveys fail to endorse cuts in many areas (including, for example in 2012, spending on the poor) is not necessarily evidence that they are "operational liberals." That concept, in short, is a tricky one, and needs to be evaluated against notions – philosophical and historical – about what conservatism means.

Endnotes

1 Lawrence R. Jacobs and Robert Y. Shapiro, "The American Public's Pragmatic Liberalism Meets Its Philosophical Conservatism," *Journal of Health Politics, Policy and Law*, No. 5 (October 1999), page 1021. See Lloyd Free and Hadley Cantril, *The Political Beliefs of Americans* (New Brunswick: Rutgers University Press, 1967) for the originators of this idea and also Christopher Ellis and James A. Stimson, *Ideology in America* (New York: Cambridge University Press, 2012), who use it extensively.
2 Hillary Rodham Clinton, *It Takes a Village* (New York: Simon and Schuster, 1996).
3 "Margaret Thatcher: a life in quotes," *The Guardian*, April 8, 2013, from an interview in *Woman's Own*, in 1987. http:www.theguardian.com/politics/2013/apr/08.
4 The relationship between the two was (gamma) .76 in 2008 and .84 in 2012.
5 See Martin Gilens, *Why Americans Hate Welfare* (Chicago: University of Chicago Press, 1999), Chapter 5, especially page 106.

5 Explaining American Conservatism
A Tale of 40 Years

An average of over 40 percent of Americans who have given a substantive answer on the American National Election Study surveys from 1972 to 2012 have thought of themselves as some type of conservative (from slightly conservative to extremely conservative). But beneath this seeming stability there has been quite a bit of movement in the correlates of conservatism over time, and it appears that change is continuing. Conservatism among members of the public may not be growing but it is evolving in ways that make it both more coherent and, in that sense, more rigid, and certainly more difficult for moderate elites to control.

This chapter looks at changes since 1972. It reprises some earlier findings, but mainly focuses on a few important questions that were asked in 1972 and also in 2008 and 2012, the latest years of the ANES surveys.[1] I also examine some areas that have not been covered so far but are important for understanding the current meaning of conservatism in the general public, for in the end what is likely to be important is not simply how many people call themselves conservatives but what that term implies for them in political and policy terms.

A Focused Overview

A central part of my argument to this point is that the conservatism that has been such a steady and prominent aspect of American public opinion for over 40 years now has gained in political significance because of a dynamic that has increased its political focus and electoral clout. It is not that we have seen a political realignment such as in the 1930s, where one dominant party (the Democrats, in this case) replaced another (the Republicans) as the dominant political force. Rather, what we see is a reorientation of politics, with conservatives in the general public identifying more and more consistently as Republicans and liberals as Democrats. This change is national in scope, but more pronounced in the American South where it has accompanied a genuine realignment in the sense that the region has gone from one dominated by Democrats (albeit often conservative Democrats) to one dominated by conservative

Republicans. More modest versions of this general phenomenon, but at the expense of Republicans, are seen in the American North in places such as New England.

From 1972 to 2008 and 2012

The 40 years covered by the ANES conservatism indicator is a period in which this measure of conservatism and its correlates tell an important story of stability and change. As just noted, while the relatively high level of conservative self-identification has remained more or less the same over time, the relationship of conservatism to party identification has

Table 5.1 Changes and Stability in the Correlates of Ideology, 1972, 2008, and 2012

Ideology Correlated with:*	1972	2008	2012
Religious Service Attendance	−.19	−.33	−.30
When Allow Abortion	−.17	−.43	−.42
Government Aid to Blacks	.34	.33	.39
Government Guarantee Jobs/ Standard of Living	.28	.37	.43

Data source: 1972, 2008, and 2012 ANES

Note: African American respondents filtered out.

*Signs of correlations vary according to direction of item answer options.

Question wordings:

Ideology measure: Where would you place YOURSELF on this scale, or haven't you thought much about this? Extremely Liberal; Liberal; Slightly Liberal; Moderate; Middle of the Road; Slightly Conservative; Conservative; Extremely Conservative.

Religious service attendance: Do you go to religious services [EVERY WEEK, ALMOST EVERY WEEK, ONCE OR TWICE A MONTH, A FEW TIMES A YEAR, or NEVER]?

Abortion, 2008 & 2012 ANES: There has been some discussion about abortion during recent years. Which one of the opinions on this page best agrees with your view? You can just tell me the number of the opinion you choose.

1 By law, abortion should never be permitted.

2 The law should permit abortion only in case of rape, incest, or when the woman's life is in danger.

3 The law should permit abortion for reasons other than rape, incest, or danger to the woman.

4 By law, a woman should always be able to obtain an abortion as a matter of personal choice.

(Note: see Table 5.3 for 1972 wording.)

Government Aid to Blacks: Seven point scale from "Government should help blacks" to "Blacks should help themselves."

Government Guarantee Jobs/Standard of Living: Seven point scale from "Government should see to jobs and standard of living" to "Government should let each person get ahead on own."

increased markedly, most especially in the South, over the same time period. Further, if we use a set of four other measures that have been employed over the relevant years of the surveys, there is evidence both of consistency and change that reveal much about what conservatism has come to mean for the individuals who profess to believe in it and for the broader polity.

Table 5.1 presents the correlations (gamma) between the four indicators and the conservatism measure in 1972, 2008 and 2012. The goal is to give a simple view of the consistency and differences in comparing the relationships 40 years ago (in 1972) and in the latest years. Somewhat more complex analysis will follow, but the straight-forward story is quite revealing.

There is clear consistency in the directions (positive or negative, depending on the direction of the answer options) of the correlation coefficients in the table over time. There were consistently negative relationships between the religious service attendance measure and favorable views of conservatism, that is, those who attended religious services most frequently (scored 1 on the religious service attendance measure) were the most likely to identify as conservatives (scored 5 to 7); and consistently negative relationships between disapproval of abortion rights (scored 1 on the when allow abortion measure) and conservatism, that is, those who felt that a woman should never be able to obtain an abortion were the most likely to identify as conservatives. And there were consistently positive relationships with measures of government aid to blacks and government guaranteed jobs and standards of living. What the former (aid to blacks) means is that those who favored government help for blacks were the most likely respondents to endorse liberalism, while those who believe that "blacks should help themselves" were most likely to favor conservatism. And the latter reflects the fact liberals are the most likely to believe that government should see to jobs and standards of living, while conservatives are most likely to endorse the idea that the government should let each person get ahead (or be left behind) without governmental guarantees.

Beyond the stability in the direction of these relationships is another clear fact. Something has happened to make religious service attendance and abortion views stronger predictors of conservatism in the most recent surveys than they were in 1972, while the correlations with ideology of views on government aid to blacks and government guarantees of jobs and standards of living, higher to begin with, remain high or, as in the guarantee of jobs and standards of living measure, have gone up from a stronger base than the relationships of professed conservatism to church attendance or abortion views.

Let's dig into these findings a bit, to see what the changes look like.

Table 5.2, a more detailed version of findings for 1972, 2008 and 2012 reported in Table 5.1, shows some modest, but revealing changes in the strength of the relationship between ideology and religious service attendance. Along with an overall drop in frequent attendance at religious services – reported weekly or almost weekly attendance fell by about 10 percentage points between 1972 and 2012 – attendance fell most notably among moderates and those who classified themselves as slightly liberal or slightly conservative. It is these figures that fueled the increase in the correlation statistics. Putnam and Campbell, in their excellent book on *Religion in American Politics*, date the increase in the relationship between religiosity and partisanship to the beginning of the 1980s.[2] In the ANES data, the growing link of religious service attendance to scores on the conservatism measure is indeed apparent in the South starting in 1980, though not so consistent in the rest of the country where the correlation statistics move around more (though generally higher starting in 1992). But the underlying point is clear; the link between religious service attendance and the ideology measure (and recall that conservatism and partisanship are increasingly linked over this period) has increased over time. Self-identified conservatives are most likely to report frequent attendance at religious services and liberals are least likely to do so, and this finding has grown stronger over time, with liberals and moderates increasingly unlikely to be frequent attenders at religious services. One stark way to say this is that the liberalism/conservatism divide is increasingly one between the secular and the religious elements in the country.

A factor that Putnam and Campbell suggest is important in the growing connection of religion to politics is the dispute over abortion.[3] And,

Table 5.2 Religious Service Attendance, Percent Attending Every Week or Almost Every Week, by Ideology, 1972, 2008, and 2012

Ideology Measure	1972	2008	2012
Extremely Liberal	17	13	22
Liberal	22	20	19
Slightly Liberal	37	23	19
Moderate	41	25	25
Slightly Conservative	49	32	35
Conservative	51	59	50
Extremely Conservative	56	65	60
Overall Percent	42	34	32
Gamma	−.19	−.33	−.30

Data source: 1972, 2008, and 2012 ANES

Note: African American respondents filtered out.

Question wording:

See Table 5.1 note.

indeed, Table 5.3 shows the level of change in the relationship between the abortion measure and scores on the liberal/conservative scale (ideology).[4] What we see are two changes: first, the support for abortion as a personal

Table 5.3 Percent Saying That Abortion Should Never Be Forbidden or Percent Endorsing Abortion as a Personal Choice,* by Ideology, 1972, 2008, and 2012

Ideology Measure	1972	2008	2012
Extremely Liberal	68	72	82
Liberal	42	73	76
Slightly Liberal	37	54	61
Moderate	25	44	44
Slightly Conservative	28	31	40
Conservative	25	20	23
Extremely Conservative	29	21	17
Overall Percent	30	40	44
Gamma	−.17	−.43	−.42

Data source: 1972, 2008, and 2012 ANES
Note: African American respondents filtered out.

*Entries are the percent favoring abortion without reservation, i.e. a woman should always be able to obtain an abortion as a matter of choice. A question wording change in 1980 and asked in both forms (compare the wordings below) led to a 10 percent increase in the percentage favoring abortion without reservation, but the correlation with the conservatism measure remained essentially the same (−.21 versus −.25).

Question wording:
Ideology measure: See Table 5.1.

Abortion, 1972 ANES: There has been some discussion about abortion during recent years. Which one of the opinions on this page best agrees with your view? You can just tell me the number of the opinion you choose.

1 Abortion should never be permitted.
2 Abortion should be permitted only if the life and health of the woman is in danger.
3 Abortion should be permitted if, due to personal reasons, the woman would have difficulty in caring for the child.
4 Abortion should never be forbidden, since one should not require a woman to have a child she doesn't want.

Abortion, 2008 & 2012 ANES: There has been some discussion about abortion during recent years. Which one of the opinions on this page best agrees with your view? You can just tell me the number of the opinion you choose.

1 By law, abortion should never be permitted.
2 The law should permit abortion only in case of rape, incest, or when the woman's life is in danger.
3 The law should permit abortion for reasons other than rape, incest, or danger to the woman.
4 By law, a woman should always be able to obtain an abortion as a matter of personal choice.

choice has risen from 30 percent in 1972 to the mid-40s in 2012; and, second, as the increased correlation coefficients suggest, those who are on the liberal end of the scale and even those in the middle of the road ("Slightly Liberal," "Moderate," or "Slightly Conservative") were far more likely to express support for abortion as a personal choice in 2008 and 2012 than in 1972, and those on the most conservative end of the scale were actually less likely to choose this option in 2008 and 2012 than in 1972. As with church attendance, the big shift in the correlation coefficients occurred in 1992.[5] Another thing worth noting is that in the latest survey in the ANES series the relationship between ideology and views on abortion is actually somewhat larger in the North than in the South.[6]

A bottom line here is that while there is more support for liberal abortion policies over time, the issue has also become more politically polarizing. While one cannot tell from cross-sectional data how individuals have changed over time, there is a good chance that the highly charged nature of the issue led some people to shift their views on conservatism to align with their position on abortion, while others may have gone the other way and shifted their position on abortion. The former seems intuitively more likely than the latter, but the Putnam and Campbell findings suggest that, when it comes to similar changes in the relationship of religious commitment and political commitment, "religious commitment, not political commitment, was more likely to change," suggesting that the latter proposition should not be dismissed out of hand.[7] In the end, though, one thing is clear: Compared to 1972, contemporary liberals (in 2008 and 2012) were more likely than liberals two generations beforehand (considering 20 years as a generation) to support abortion as a personal choice as are moderates, but conservatives have bucked this trend becoming, if anything, more opposed to abortion as a personal choice than were conservatives 40 years before. And, overall, the issue has gone from mildly polarizing to very polarizing as it has become what it was not before: a belief that tends to separate clearly liberals and conservatives.

When it comes to government assistance to blacks, opinion has changed towards a more restrictive view of the government's role, although the relationship with ideology has changed very little (see Table 5.4). I should stress that this question, chosen because it is common across the years, does not ask about racial integration or discrimination in housing or public facilities, but about the general proposition that "government should help blacks" as one end of a seven-point scale and that "blacks should help themselves" as the other end. Whereas in 1972, almost a third of the non-black population surveyed fell somewhere on the government should aid blacks end of the scale, by 2012 the percentage had fallen to 13. And, I should note, this change is not due to a flow of opinion into the middle (4) category. The percentages in categories 5–7, those falling towards the "blacks should help themselves" end of the continuum, went from about 43 percent in 1972 to about 60 percent

Table 5.4 Percent in Favor* of Government Assistance to Blacks, by Ideology, 1972, 2008, and 2012

Ideology Measure	1972	2008	2012
Extremely Liberal	65	66	51
Liberal	58	42	34
Slightly Liberal	54	22	20
Moderate	28	11	12
Slightly Conservative	24	8	8
Conservative	15	10	3
Extremely Conservative	14	7	3
Overall Percent	32	17	13
Gamma	.34	.33	.39

Data source: 1972, 2008, and 2012 ANES

Note: African American respondents filtered out.

*Percent in favor includes those placing themselves 1-3 on a 7 point scale where 1 anchors the supportive end ("Government should help blacks") and 7 anchors the opposition end ("Blacks should help themselves").

Question wording:

Ideology measure: See Table 5.1 note.

Government assistance to blacks: Some people feel that the government in Washington should make every effort to improve the social and economic position of blacks. (Suppose these people are at one end of a scale, at point 1.) Others feel that the government should not make any special effort to help blacks because they should help themselves. (Suppose these people are at the other end, at point 7.) And, of course, some other people have opinions somewhere in between, at points 2, 3, 4, 5, or 6. Where would you place yourself on this scale, or haven't you thought much about this?

in 2008 and about 63 percent to 2012. But the relationship with the ideology measure remained at approximately the same level in the years in the table (rising a bit in 2012) because support for the idea that government should help blacks dropped for liberals and for conservatives. So, to take one example, support for government assistance to blacks for the "Extremely Liberal" fell from 65 percent to 51 percent and, for the "Extremely Conservative," it fell from 14 percent to 3 percent. The drop was even greater for those in the center of the ideology measure, especially the "Slightly Liberal."

Finally, Table 5.5, examines the relationship between ideology and a 7-point scale that goes from "government should see to jobs and standards of living" (1) to "government should let each person get ahead on own" (7). Unlike the previous scale that has a clear racial referent, responses to this one have remained relatively the same over the years, but the relationship of scores on the scale to ideological self-placement has shown a marked increase. (The correlations between ideology and

Table 5.5 Percent in Favor* of Government Guarantee of Jobs and Living Standards, by Ideology, 1972, 2008, and 2012

Ideology Measure	1972	2008	2012
Extremely Liberal	64	79	70
Liberal	55	50	43
Slightly Liberal	32	49	40
Moderate	23	26	32
Slightly Conservative	19	15	20
Conservative	15	14	10
Extremely Conservative	17	3	8
Overall Percent	26	25	27
Gamma	.28	.37	.43

Data source: 1972, 2008, and 2012 ANES
Note: African American respondents filtered out.

*Percent in favor includes those placing themselves 1-3 on a 7 point scale where 1 anchors the supportive end ("Government should see to jobs and standards of living") and 7 anchors the opposition end ("Government should let each person get ahead on own").

Question wording:
Ideology measure: See Table 5.1.

Government guarantee of jobs and living standards: Where would you place YOURSELF on this scale, or haven't you thought much about this?

scores on the scale were close to the 1972 figure (.28) for most years in the ANES surveys; then, in 2004, they increase to the levels shown in 2008 and 2012.)

A look inside Table 5.5 suggests that the changes in the correlations come from a small increase in endorsement of the notion that the government should see to jobs and standards of living among the most liberal and a decrease in that same sentiment among the most conservative who, as the table makes clear, were already very skeptical about this notion of government responsibility. Again, it is important to stress that these figures indicate an increase in the differentiation of the views of those who call themselves liberals or conservatives, but, unlike the fall in support for government aid to blacks, support for government guarantees of jobs and income has stayed the same, although at a low level.

So what these data tell us so far is that the ties between ideology and indicators of religiosity, views on abortion, views on race (whether the government should assist blacks), and, finally, an indicator of economic ideology suggest a marked relationship to conservatism and, for all of the variables but one (the racial measure, that was robust to begin with), relationships that are clearly stronger in the contemporary period than they were in 1972. And, relatedly, one can say that contemporary conservatives

are more religious than non-conservatives (specifically, they are more frequent attenders at religious services),[8] less likely to endorse a woman's
right to choose when it comes to abortion policy, less likely to favor
government help for blacks, and more likely to think that the each person
should get ahead on his or her own rather than relying on government
guarantees of jobs or provision of an adequate standard of living.

As noted, these variables were chosen for this part of the analysis
because they are available starting in 1972 as well as in more recent
years and a major purpose of this chapter is to examine in greater detail
than before what has occurred to make ideology, a variable whose distribution has not changed much in the years covered, so much more
politically potent over time. In pursuit of that goal, the next section looks
at how much of the variance in scores on the conservatism measure can
be explained by these predictors, particularly how much change has
occurred over time in the explanatory power of a simple model.

Table 5.6 Explaining American Conservatism: A Tale of 40 Years

Year and Sample Included	Multiple R*	Adjusted R2*
1972		
Total	.441	.192
Non-College Graduate	.380	.141
College Graduate	.621	.375
2008		
Total	.598	.352
Non-College Graduate	.513	.254
College Graduate	.755	.558
2012		
Total	.604	.364
Non-College Graduate	.539	.289
College Graduate	.706	.497

Data source: 1972, 2008, and 2012 ANES
Note: African American Respondents filtered out.
*Variables: Dependent: Ideology (Liberal/conservative) measure
              Independent: When should abortion be allowed
                           Religious service attendance
                           Government aid to blacks
                           Government guaranteed jobs/standard of living
Question wording:
See Table 5.1 to 5.5 notes.

The Difference a Few Decades Make

Table 5.6 displays a pared-down version of the results (Multiple R's and Adjusted R's Squared) of multiple regression analyses with ideology as the dependent variable and the four variables previously examined in the chapter (see the list in Table 5.1) as the independent variables. In each year, the analyses were done for all respondents (except African Americans, as per earlier discussions) and for college graduates and those who have not graduated from college separately. The two educational levels were selected to demonstrate a difference that is consistent in these data and in the literature on ideology and, indeed, attitude studies in general – that is, greater structure and consistency of views among the better educated.

The first thing to take note of is that while the four variables explained a respectable 19.2 percent of the variance (an Adjusted R-squared of .192) in scores on the ideology measure for the respondents in 1972, the percentage rose to 35.2 of variance explained in 2008 and to 36.4 in 2012. These are very strong findings for survey data – and, I should stress, there was no manipulation to transform any of the scores – and are especially strong because the particular independent variables were chosen on the simple basis of continuity across the studies. Other, and possibly better measures of the same concepts (particularly religiosity) that we know are related to conservatism might well have yielded even stronger results, though a test I did using a variable measuring beliefs about whether the Bible is the literal word of God yielded only very modestly changed results.[9] So, on the basis of these four independent variables alone, we know that we can understand a lot about conservatism. In short, just by considering views on abortion (which incidentally, in accord with the data presented earlier in this chapter, was not a statistically significant predictor in 1972 – though it was close – for either college graduates or for those who had not gotten a college degree[10]), frequency of attendance at religious services, and views on government assistance to African Americans and on whether or not the government should provide a guarantee of jobs and standard of living for the populace we can by 2008 explain more than a third of the variance in our ideology measure for most of the general population.[11]

A closer look at the results controlling for education is also revealing. First, the increase in variance explained is consistently higher for college graduates than for non-college graduates. Education, as one would expect, matters. The highly educated are more likely than those who have less education to see links between their beliefs and their views on a variety of political issues and their ideological positioning. But that said, Table 5.6 also shows how much more tightly linked the set of variables in the table and ideology have become for both groups over time. As part of the general reconfiguration of politics analyzed in Chapter 2, the population now has a set of beliefs that are more predictably related to their identification as conservatives or liberals, that is, to their expressed ideology, and arguably more coherent than they were years ago. That does not necessarily make for an improved politics, but it does contribute to stronger divisions in political life.

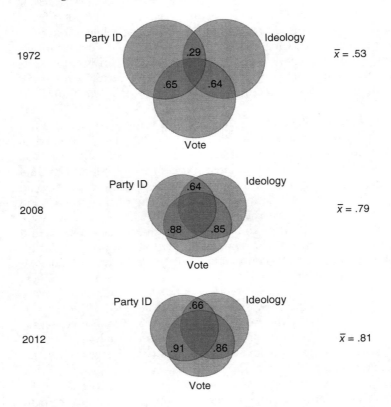

Figure 5.1 The Closing Circle of Ideology: Party, Ideology, and the Two-Party Vote for President

Data Source: 1972–2012 ANES

African American respondents filtered out.

Note: Areas of overlap between circles illustrate the bivariate correlations between variables. The convergence of circles over time represents the increasing average correlation for all variables. Note that the amount of overlap *approximates* the corresponding numerical correlations.

*Including the effect of third party candidates changes the average correlations only slightly: 1980 = .56; 1992 = .63; 1996 = .71. In short, the basic pattern holds.

The Closing Circle of Ideology

Part of the predictability and coherence is evident in what I call here "the closing circle of ideology." Recall from Chapter 2 that the links between ideology and party identification have gotten stronger over time, especially in the South, but also in the rest of the country. Now look at Figure 5.1. The figure shows the correlations (gamma) between measures of party identification (Strong Democrat = 1 through to Strong Republican = 7), vote choice between the two major candidates for president (Democrat = 1 and Republican = 2) and the measure of ideology we have used throughout this study ("Extremely Liberal" = 1 to "Extremely Conservative" = 7) arranged in a figure, with the data for 1972 at the top, followed by 2008 and then 2012 at the bottom.[12] The smaller the area of the figure, the greater the overlap between the variables; perfect overlap (a correlation of 1.0 between all three variables) would be represented by a simple circle.

What the data in the figure show is that party, ideology and vote are more and more closely linked over time. The mean correlation between the three measures was .53 in 1972 and rose slowly over the ensuing years (averaging .64 from 1976 to 2000)[13] to 2004 where it stabilized at around .80.[14] The dynamics inside these averages are well represented in the circles in Figure 5.1. Each coefficient is up between 1972 and 2008 or 2012, with the relationship between party identification and ideology showing the largest increases, but with the other relationships, those between party identification and vote and vote and ideology, up also, although not as much. In short, tell me a person's party identification and I can not only do a somewhat better job now of predicting his or her vote than I might have previously, but I can also do a much better job of predicting his or her ideology. And if I know a person's ideology score, I can tell you how that person voted (or, to be more precise, how the person says that he or she voted). There is a closing circle of partisan identification, vote choice and ideological identification that has occurred over the years, one that exemplifies the reshaping of politics in the United States.

Assorted Other Elements of Contemporary American Conservatism

There are assorted other issues not covered so far that define or have come to define American conservatism.

One issue of long-standing importance for conservatives is the national defense. While conservatives often disapprove of government spending in the abstract, and they are certainly more skeptical than liberals about government money spent on others whom they may feel are undeserving or even harmed by publicly funded benefits such as welfare, they regard national defense as a major public good. This is apparent in the ANES data, though the questions on defense spending are not consistent across the years. In the 1970s, ANES asked about cutting military spending or continuing it at its (then) present level. Those identifying as conservatives consistently, and by large majorities, favored at least continuing defense spending at present levels. In 1972, for example, while well over 70 percent of those at the liberal end of the spectrum ("Extremely Liberal," or "Liberal" on the scale) favored cutting military spending, over 80 percent of those at the conservative end of the scale ("Conservative" or "Extremely Conservative") favored continuing defense spending at least at current levels. (The gamma coefficient is .41.) Similar results held in 1976 (gamma = .41), although with stronger support for defense spending among liberals in that post-Vietnam year. The defense spending item was revised starting in 1980 to a seven-point scale (going from decrease defense spending to increase defense spending), and the relationship with ideology averaged slightly below .30 for the next few rounds of interviewing, but it was back up above .40 in 2004 and has averaged close to that (.37) since then. In short, conservatives want to increase defense spending and liberals want to decrease it, and this basic finding is quite robust.

Many other issues and values separate contemporary conservatives and liberals, but the ANES data series do not always allow for analyses over time. My guess is that all of them would, like abortion and religiosity, have differentiated liberals and conservatives to a certain extent at

Table 5.7 Percent in Favor of Making It More Difficult to Buy a Gun, by Ideology, 2008 and 2012

Ideology	Percentage in Favor of Making It More Difficult to Buy a Gun	
	2008	2012
Extremely Liberal	72.3	74.7
Liberal	58.8	70.5
Slightly Liberal	49.5	59.9
Moderate	43.1	48.7
Slightly Conservative	41.4	38.7
Conservative	32.4	20.4
Extremely Conservative	25.1	17.9
Overall Percent	43	44
Gamma	.27	.44

Data source: 2008 and 2012 ANES

Note: African American Respondents filtered out.

Question wording:.

Ideology measure: See Table 5.1 note.

Difficulty in buying a gun: Do you think the federal government should make it MORE DIFFICULT for people to buy a gun than it is now, make it EASIER for people to buy a gun, or KEEP THESE RULES ABOUT THE SAME as they are now?

Recoded to: (1) More difficult; (2) Keep the rules about the same; (3) Make it easier.

each point in time, but as with abortion and religion, the relationship of several of them with ideology may have increased over time.

One example might be gun control (Table 5.7). Here we see an increase in the relationship between support for rules making it more difficult to buy or own a gun and ideology, one that has grown even in the period between 2008 and 2012, something typical of the spending variables discussed in Chapter 4. In 2008, a little more than half of the public favored federal policies to make it more difficult for people to buy a gun than was the case at the time, with most of the rest of the opinion that the rules should remain the same. (Less than 4 percent wanted the rules eased.) Those figures did not change much in the 2012 survey.

However, as noted above, what did increase was the strength of the relationship between ideology and views on gun control. The 2008 survey followed the 2008 Supreme Court ruling that federal law could not restrict the right to gun ownership in the home for self-defense (District of Columbia v. Heller), a ruling that was extended to states and localities in a 2010 case (McDonald v. City of Chicago). As the decisions became more and more a subject of debate, the relationship between ideology and support for rules to make gun ownership more difficult increased. In 2008 (and, again, these findings do not include African Americans who are the racial group most in favor of gun control), the correlation between ideology and the gun control measure was .27, with about 72 percent of those calling themselves "Extremely Liberal" favoring making it more difficult to buy a gun, but with the percentage holding that view falling to 59 percent for "Liberals" and to just a bit below 50 percent for the "Slightly Liberal." Large majorities of conservatives of all types wanted the rules kept the same or even made easier (20 percent of the "Extremely Conservative" were in the latter – easier – group). By 2012, the relationship between the two variables had jumped to (gamma) .44. Liberals of all types were more likely to favor more difficult rules (even 60 percent of the "Slightly Liberal"), while conservatives went more in the other direction. These findings, as noted in the previous paragraph, follow a general trend of strengthening relationships in 2012 as compared to 2008, so one cannot be sure of the impact of the Supreme Court cases, but the increased link of conservatism to views on gun control is indisputable.

Opinion on the pace of progress in ensuring equal rights in the US also shows continuity and, in this case, slight evidence of a strengthening relationship with conservatism. Table 5.8 presents the data. The correlation between ideology and views on whether the US has "gone too far pushing equal rights" increased from –.35 to –.44, not a great increase, but one in line with other changes showing that the potency of identification as a liberal or conservative is growing stronger. Two facts about the table stand out, at least for my purposes here: 1. The increase in the gamma statistic clearly comes from a modest but consistent increase in the percentage of those who are on the conservative end of the spectrum and express strong or modified agreement with the proposition that the

Table 5.8 Have We Gone Too Far Pushing Equal Rights in This Country, by Ideology, 2008 and 2012

Ideology	Percentage Agree Push Too Far*	
	2008	2012
Extremely Liberal	7.8	7.8
Liberal	11.7	12.5
Slightly Liberal	17.9	22.4
Moderate	33.3	30.4
Slightly Conservative	40.2	46.5
Conservative	50.3	58.4
Extremely Conservative	60.1	67.9
Overall Percent	35.9	37.3
Gamma	−.35	−.44

Data source: 2008 and 2012 ANES

Note: African Americans respondents filtered out.

*Entries are percentage who "agree strongly" or "agree somewhat" with the statement.

Question wording:

Ideology measure: See Table 5.1 note.

Equal rights too far: 'We have gone too far in pushing equal rights in this country.'

(Do you AGREE STRONGLY, AGREE SOMEWHAT, NEITHER AGREE NOR DISAGREE, DISAGREE SOMEWHAT, or DISAGREE STRONGLY with this statement?)

US has gone too far in this direction; and 2. The rather strong hold that this proposition has on conservatives in a population that, overall, does not agree strongly or even somewhat with this notion. This example of those with relatively strong conservative leanings tending to be out of sync with mainstream opinion in some issue areas is a subject that will come up again as we consider the future prospects for conservatism in the final chapter of this volume.

Health care was an issue that found full expression in the 2012 election after passage of the Affordable Care Act in 2010, and conservatives and liberals were extraordinarily divided in their views. Table 5.9 is a simple presentation showing how greatly different conservatives and liberals were in their evaluations of this act (Obamacare, as it became known, partly because the President himself embraced the term). "Extremely Conservative" and "Conservative" people gave the law almost no support as contrasted to well more than 70 percent of "Extremely Liberal" and "Liberal" identifiers. One could argue that Obamacare was such a partisan issue that the .58 correlation with ideology is simply a reflection of that fact, and to a degree it is. However, controlling for the individual's party identification does not eliminate the relationship (though it does reduce the correlation to an average of .32), so there is more at work here than simply partisanship.

Table 5.9 Percent in Favor* of The Affordable Care Act, by Ideology, 2012

Ideology	Percent in Favor of Affordable Care Act
Extremely Liberal	76.7
Liberal	79.1
Slightly Liberal	59.1
Moderate	33.0
Slightly Conservative	23.0
Conservative	8.3
Extremely Conservative	5.5
Overall Percent	34.1
Gamma	.58

Data source: 2012 ANES
Note: African American Respondents filtered out.

*Percent in favor includes those placing themselves 1-3 (Favor a great deal; Favor moderately; Favor a little) on a 7 point scale. Relatively few respondents were in the "Favor a little" category.

Question wording:
Ideology measure: See Table 5.1 note.

Affordable Care Act: Do you favor, oppose, or neither favor nor oppose the health care reform law passed in 2010? This law requires all Americans to buy health insurance and requires health insurance companies to accept everyone. Do you favor that [a great deal, moderately, or a little/a little, moderately, or a great deal]?

A last example is immigration, a big issue for Republicans, the party of conservatives, if they are to improve their standing with the growing Latino population. There is a strong relationship between ideology and the views of respondents on "illegal" immigration ("undocumented" immigration is the term now used by those who are sympathetic to the plight of the immigrants who live in the US without legal authorization). The lack of sympathy on the part of conservatives was manifested in the 2008 ANES when respondents were asked about the importance of controlling "illegal" immigration. (The question was not asked in 2012.) Liberals, as Table 5.10 makes clear, are relatively unconcerned about this, but conservatives are very concerned. This issue played out in the 2008 and 2012 elections, and will almost certainly be a factor in the 2016 election, and dealing with it has vexed many Republican leaders who would like to address issues related to it in hopes of increasing their support among Latinos.

Conclusion

While the level of conservatism in the general public has not changed much between 1972 and 2012, its significance has. Whether a person

Table 5.10 Importance of Controlling Illegal Immigration as a US Policy Goal, Percent "Very Important" by Ideology, 2008

Ideology Measure	Percent Illegal Immigration Control Very Important
Extremely Liberal	11.9
Liberal	28.8
Slightly Liberal	46.2
Moderate	61.2
Slightly Conservative	60.3
Conservative	71.7
Extremely Conservative	77.6
Overall Percent	56.6
Gamma	−.41

Data source: 2008 ANES
Note: African American Respondents filtered out.

Question wording:
Ideology measure: See Table 5.1 note.
Controlling illegal immigration: Should CONTROLLING AND REDUCING ILLEGAL IMMIGRATION be a VERY IMPORTANT foreign policy goal, a SOMEWHAT IMPORTANT foreign policy goal, or NOT AN IMPORTANT foreign policy goal at all?

identifies as a conservative or a liberal (and the degree to which he or she identifies) has increasing significance for the party the person identifies with for his or her vote. The rough generalizations of four decades ago are still true, only much more so. Liberal identifiers are now more predictably Democrats and conservatives, especially in the South, but also throughout the country, are more predictably Republicans. What we have seen is not realignment in the sense of a changed majority, but rather a reconfiguration of the relationships between conservatism, vote and party that has made voters more consistent and coherent in their beliefs and voting choices, but has left politics more divided.

Further, the relationship between issue attitudes and ideology has increased over time. This can be seen most pointedly in the increase in variance explained over time in the regressions analyses in the chapter using the same predictor variables. The predictors of conservatism in 1972 continued to predict in 2008 and 2012, only they predict even better. This is part of the strengthening of the conservative belief system, complementing the convergence of ideology, party, and vote in the US and of a piece with the strong relationships between ideology and the other beliefs examined in this chapter and in Chapters 3 and 4.

What we see, as of 2012, is a conservatism that is strongly related to religiosity, beliefs about abortion, economic attitudes, and views about race. Each of these factors has an independent effect on ideology, and together they have a greater impact on ideology than they did 40 years previously, in 1972. In short, contemporary ideology not only is closely tied to the party identification and voting behavior of individuals today, but is evidently deeply rooted in personal beliefs and practices.

The public is increasingly split along ideological grounds, in some instances to a ludicrous degree. For example, the ANES asked respondents in 2012 whether they thought President Obama was born in the United States. Though a certified copy of President Obama's original birth certificate had already been released (and contemporaneous newspaper announcements of his birth were also available) in an effort to finally counter the strong rumors in conservative circles about the place of his birth, the correlation between ideology and the belief that Obama might not have been born in the US in 2012 was (gamma) .49. While over 80 percent of those describing themselves as "Extremely Liberal" or "Liberal" thought he was definitely born in the United States, that figure fell below 20 percent for those identifying as "Conservative" or "Extremely Conservative," and was only 11 percent for the latter (though 23 percent of the extremely conservative conceded that he was "probably" born in the US). The late Senator Daniel Patrick Moynihan is often quoted to the effect that while we are all entitled to our own opinions, we are not entitled to our own facts. Maybe not, but ideological identification is apparently strong enough among a significant proportion of the American public to blur the line between the two to a large extent.

Endnotes

1 I used these years to keep the data presentations simple, but still show change. In a few cases, however, I use the available data from more than the 1972, 2008 and 2012 surveys, and sometimes, particularly at the end of the chapter where the emphasis is on areas not previously discussed, I focus in on either a comparison of 2008 and 2012 or even on 2012 alone.
2 Robert D. Putnam and David E. Campbell, *American Grace: How Religion Divides and United Us* (New York: Simon and Schuster, 2010), especially pages 387–388.
3 Putnam and Campbell, *American Grace* (2010), pages 388–396.
4 The two (religiosity and abortion), while strongly related, are distinguishable in the minds of the respondents. In 2012, for example, the relationship (gamma) between religious service attendance and abortion attitudes was .48.
5 I should note here that the wording of the abortion item was modified somewhat in 1980. Both the old and newer versions were tested in that year. Correlations with the ideology question were quite similar for both versions and in line with the findings described in the text.
6 The gamma coefficients in 2012 are –.36 for the South and –.45 for the North (rest of the country), produced by slightly greater percentages of Northern liberals who support abortion as a matter of choice and very slightly smaller proportions of Northern conservatives than Southern conservatives who endorse abortion as a matter of personal choice. (Incidentally, in 1972 the coefficients were low in both regions in keeping with the low figure in Table 5.1.)

7 Putnam and Campbell, *American Grace* (2010), page 145.

8 Other indicators of religiosity show similar results. Religious service attendance, like the other variables discussed so far, was chosen because data are available for all of the relevant years.

9 This variable was not used in the 1972 survey. It was, however, employed, starting in 1980, with a slight modification in wording over the time period. The question was the same in 2008 and 2012, with respondents given a choice between 1. The Bible is the actual word of God and is to be taken liberally word for word; 2. The Bible is the word of God but not everything in it should be taken literally, word for word; and 3. The Bible is a book written by men and is not the word of God. With that variable in the 2008 and 2012 equations as a substitute for religious service attendance, the amount of variance explained is 36.0 percent in 2008 and 38.3 percent in 2012, figures almost exactly the same as with the religious service attendance variable. (And, not surprisingly, there is a very strong correlation between the Bible and religious service attendance variables.)

10 Aside from Putnam and Campbell, *American Grace* (2010), particularly pages 388–396 (especially page 392 on "the time it took for evangelical leaders to embrace the pro-life cause as fully as their Catholic counterparts"), see William Martin, *With God on Our Side; The Rise of the Religious Right in America* (New York: Broadway Books, 1996), especially pages 192–196.

11 As mentioned in this paragraph, the abortion variable was not statistically significant (.05) in any of the 1972 regressions, but it was significant in all of the 2008 and 2012 regressions. In addition, religious service attendance did not reach the .05 significance level for the non-college graduate regression in 2008.

12 Data for all presidential years from 1972 to 2012 are arrayed across the bottom of the figure.

13 These data do not include 1992 and 1996 when there was a significant vote for a third party candidate (Ross Perot), making a strict comparison to the other years impossible. However, the data show the same trends.

14 I ran regressions for each presidential year with the same variables used in Table 5.6 and the adjusted R-squared stabilized in 2004 (at 0.356), near the high levels reported for 2008 and 2012.

6 How Different Are Political Elites and the Public?

My main focus up to this point in the book has been on the views of the public. But in this chapter I take advantage of data from a unique study that allows us to examine precisely (or at least as precisely as survey measures permit) the similarities and differences between political elites and the public. My aim is to take a step beyond an earlier examination I did using these data in order to see just how much difference there is between elites and the public when one looks a little deeper into the composition of the public, that is, in this case, once one controls for the level of education of the public.[1] The results need to be understood in the context of a set of issues roiling the public debate as well as the political science literature: How polarized are politics in the US? Is polarization mainly an elite phenomenon? If so, how should we characterize what is going on in American society at large?

Polarization

Polarization is the subject of an intense debate in the political science literature. There is little doubt that the parties in Congress have become increasingly polarized. Sean Theriault, for example, in his book on *Party Polarization in Congress* summarizes a large literature showing, based on a variety of studies using indicators based on voting in Congress such as interest group ratings and roll call measures like the famous DW-NOMINATE scores, "that Democrats have become more liberal and Republicans have become more conservative since the 1970s."[2] Indeed, whereas in the 1970s there was quite a bit of overlap in the voting scores of Republicans and Democrats, by the early 2000s that overlap had just about disappeared. Further, Theriault concludes, that "although the southern states have been leading the trend, northern states have not been immune from it" and "although the majority of the polarization has resulted from ideological members replacing more moderate members, congressional veterans have not been immune to the party polarization that surrounds them."[3]

As I said above, these basic facts are not in dispute. But there are substantial disagreements about the causes of the polarization in Congress and, relatedly, how much the polarization reflects changes in the electorate or is itself a major cause of change in the electorate. Some of the polarization comes from the growth of Republican Party strength in the South, but since the phenomenon is more widespread than that, it can only be a partial explanation at best. The growth and effectiveness of conservative think tanks is another factor that has influenced trends in the party, and especially among its elected officials, and that certainly has had some impact.[4] Reactions to social changes as varied as voting rights for Southern blacks and the various movements that gained energy in the 1960s and afterwards, such as women's liberation and gay rights, has clearly had some impact – recall, for example, the greater conservatism of married women and widows compared to their single or divorced counterparts, or the growing import of attitudes towards abortion on whether or not a person identifies as a conservative (and, as the links to voting show, votes for the Republican Party). Another factor is clearly the growing links of religiosity to voting.

All of the factors just mentioned, and more, have been important in dividing the country ideologically and could logically be causes of polarization in elite politics generally and in Congress in particular. However, there is another way to look at this that is identified with the work of Morris Fiorina and his associates. They argue, in brief, that rather than *following* voters, elites "are imposing their own agendas on voters."[5] Voters' behavior is being driven by the repositioning of elites. An example would be the changing relationship between religiosity and party identification, where, Fiorina et al. argue, the changing correlation between religiosity and party identification may reflect changes in party positions more than changes in voter attitudes.[6]

The core of the argument is that a form of "sorting" has taken place. Voters see party leaders taking positions on issues that they both did not emphasize before nor expressed their positions on in moderate form, and voters begin to sort themselves out accordingly over time. Further, "when a voter sorts, he brings his issue positions into alignment with one another – his attitudes become more consistent with one another. As a result, the mass parties become more internally homogeneous. While this process has limits (e.g., it does not create an electorate of sophisticated ideologues), it does make the distribution of opinion within the within the party more homogenous . . . [And] more homogenous within-party distributions of opinion give candidates incentives to move away from the center either to win a primary election or to avoid a challenge altogether."[7]

This is an appealing argument, in part because it lays the blame (assuming, for the moment that polarization is a bad thing) on the elite. To fix the problem, what we would need is a better elite, and hard as that might be to arrange it is probably easier than arranging for a better public. Reforming the primary system, non-partisan redistricting, public financing of elections, and various tax law changes are just a few of the things that one might imagine doing. But, for now, those things are not on the immediate horizon, so I want to look more closely at the question of how much more polarized elites are than their fellow citizens. In particular, I want to see whether the degree of polarization by ideology is greater among elites than it is among the public at large once one takes into account something as basic as the different educational levels of the elite and the general public. If it is greater, especially if the gap is large for the elites and modest for roughly comparable members of the public, that would reinforce the notion that elites are "imposing" their agendas on the public. If the differences are large and about the same in the comparable public, that would either suggest that elites have succeeded in polarizing a significant part of the polity as it has "sorted" itself out or that the same forces that have driven the parties apart have also driven the public apart and, parenthetically, that change may be quite difficult to accomplish, even if reforms of the type listed above are enacted.

The Institutions of American Democracy Study

Ordinarily, it is very difficult to compare the views of elites and the public in a precise way. We have the votes and speeches of legislators and the statements of officials, for example, but we rarely have their answers to the same questions we might pose of a sample of the general public. In fact, getting a representative sample of any part of the political elite to answer standard survey questions is a difficult task. And it follows that getting enough interviews from samples of several elements of the political elite is a major undertaking.[8]

However, in 2004–2005 the Annenberg Foundation Trust at Sunnylands sponsored a study as part of the Institutions of American Democracy Project and conducted by Princeton Research Associates International that resulted in comparable surveys of the general public, staff members in congressional offices, political appointees who had served in the Clinton administration and appointees in the then current Bush administration, and career officials in the Senior Executive Service.[9]

The respondents were asked to answer many of the same questions, so there are data that compare, in a precise way, the views of the public and those of important parts of the political elite at a time when we know that the polarization/sorting of both Congress and the public had reached high levels. The items are not perfect for the purpose I have at hand, but they are quite useful in answering the questions posed above about the degree of difference between the views of conservatives and liberals.

The focus of the relevant questions in the Annenberg study was on how much responsibility the federal government should have for doing six listed things (the list was randomized in the administration of the survey). The responsibilities were: 1. Conserving the country's natural resources; 2. Keeping taxes low; 3. Protecting the unborn; 4. Promoting stronger morals; 5. Promoting racial equality; and 6. Reducing poverty.[10] Conservatives and liberals have been debating about government responsibilities in these areas for years, although some have obviously been more contentious than others.

The Annenberg study respondents were also asked a question about their political views quite comparable to the liberal/conservative question in the ANES. Answer categories were: Very Conservative; Conservative; Moderate; Liberal; Very Liberal.[11]

How Different Are They?

Starting with ideology, the distribution for the Annenberg survey public respondents on the ideology scale used in the instrument is quite congruent with the results in the ANES surveys. Conservatives (the sum of those answering "Conservative" or "Very Conservative") have a plurality (roughly 41 percent of the responses), followed closely by moderates (roughly 40 percent) and more than double the percentage of self-identified liberals.[12]

The other samples fell out about as one might expect, with the exception perhaps of the sample of top career civil servants.[13] Since the congressional survey focused on the staff in congressional offices (in an attempt to find people who would reasonably be expected to mirror the views of the members in whose offices they worked), the respondents are split in their ideological views (staffers for Democrats more liberal and those of Republicans more conservative), although the plurality of moderates suggests somewhat less division than might have been expected. Political appointees fall out neatly into the right-leaning emphasis of the George W. Bush appointees and the center to left emphasis of the Clinton administration. The most unexpected result was in the answers of the career civil servants, particularly in the larger than expected percentage of moderates. Previous research, though not using the same measure, indicated a smaller percentage of centrists in the top US career bureaucracy (and a larger percentage leaning left), although it also suggested a rightward drift in the top career bureaucracy in the late 1980s and early 1990s when Republican presidents were in office.[14]

The data on views of government responsibilities revealed gaps between the views of liberal and conservatives as well as differences across samples and differences across issues.[15]

Conservatives, no matter which sample one looks at, were more likely to think it very important or important to keep taxes low, protect the unborn, and promote stronger morals than liberals. That is not a huge surprise, given what we've seen so far in this book, nor is the fact that the gaps between conservatives and liberals are greater for the various elite groups than for general public as a whole. Conservatives were also likely to endorse the ideal that it is the federal government's responsibility to conserve the nation's natural resources, promote racial equality and reduce poverty, but they tended not to see these things as very important responsibilities (as to simply important responsibilities) while liberals were much more likely to put a priority on such things.

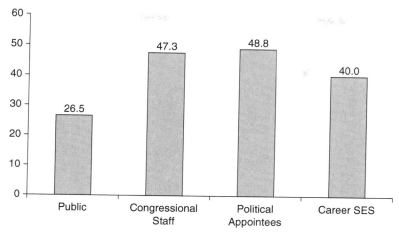

Figure 6.1 Conservatives and Liberals: Average Gap between Them on Government Responsibilities,* 2004–2005

Data Source: Calculated from Tables 3.1 and 3.2 (pages 51 and 52) found in Joel D. Aberbach "The Future of The American Right," in Joel D. Aberbach and Gillian Peele, editors, *Crisis of Conservatism?* (New York: Oxford University Press, 2011). The data are from the Institution of American Democracy Project survey sponsored by the Annenberg Foundation Trust at Sunnylands and available through the Annenberg Public Policy Center web site.

Note: African American respondents filtered out.

*Bars represent average percentage differences between self-identified conservatives and liberals in each sample on the responsibilities of the federal government. The differences were calculated using "very important" or "important" for the federal government to keep taxes low, protect the unborn and promote stronger morals (all areas which conservatives are more likely to see as government responsibility) and "very important" for government to conserve the country's natural resources, promote racial equality and reduce poverty (all areas where liberals are more likely to indicate a government responsibility).

Question wording:

Ideology measure: Where would you place YOURSELF on this scale, or haven't you thought much about this? Extremely Liberal; Liberal; Slightly Liberal; Moderate; Middle of the Road; Slightly Conservative; Conservative; Extremely Conservative.

Federal government responsibilities: I now want to ask you some questions about how much responsibility the federal government should have for doing certain things. In your opinion, how important is it for the federal government to do each of the following? Is [Insert] a very important responsibility of the federal government, important, not so important or not important at all? What about [Insert].

a Keeping taxes low
b Protecting the unborn
c Promoting stronger morals
d Conserving the country's natural resources
e Promoting racial equality
f Reducing poverty

There was greater consensus in the areas where federal government responsibilities are more likely to be favored by liberals than conservatives. These areas – conserving the country's natural resources, promoting

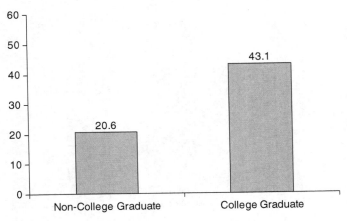

Figure 6.2 Conservatives and Liberals in the Public: Average Gap between Them on Government Responsibilities,* by Education Level, 2004–2005

Data source: The Institution of American Democracy Project survey sponsored by the Annenberg Foundation Trust at Sunnylands and available through the Annenberg Public Policy Center web site

Note: African American respondents filtered out.

*See Figure 6.1 note.

racial equality, and reducing poverty – turn out to have greater common agreement than issues like taxes, protecting the unborn, and the promotion of stronger morals, and better fit the philosophical conservative and operational liberal hypotheses discussed in Chapter 5, but there is still a clear difference between liberals and conservatives as reflected in the priorities they place on these things, that is, in the percentages who regard these as "very important" (as opposed to "important") responsibilities of the federal government.

Figure 6.1, calculated from the data in Tables 3.1 and 3.2 of "The Future of the American Right," presents the average gap in the absolute values of the differences between conservatives and liberals with respect to respondents' beliefs about the federal government's responsibilities.[16] The figure makes clear, as expected, that the elites are more divided by ideology than the general public and that the career SES (Senior Executive Service) is the least divided in this respect among the governmental elite groups.

However, this does not tell the entire story. A simple control dividing the public sample into those who have graduated from college and those who have not, tells a more subtle tale. College graduates look remarkably like members of the governmental elite. A look at Figure 6.2 shows that the gap between college-educated liberals and conservatives on beliefs about the responsibilities of government falls between the gaps for congressional staff and political appointees, on the one hand, and members of the career SES on the other. Put another way, the 43.1 percent gap for the college educated is only a whisper less than the 45.4 percent average gaps between conservatives and liberals for the three elite groups.

These findings on differences between the public and American elites are consistent with work such as that found in the classic paper on belief systems in mass publics by Philip Converse, showing large differences between constraints on attitudes of a cross-section of the population and congressional candidates using 1958 ANES data (plus analysis indicating that more sophisticated, generally better educated, members of the public are those most likely to have a coherent belief structure).[17] Many other studies emphasize the importance of conceptual levels in the general public, with education as a proxy variable for sophistication.[18] Two things are clear: 1. We know that contemporary voters are much less confused than their predecessors might have been about whether or not they are conservatives or liberals, that is, when asked the same question a few months apart, they answer the same way, suggesting at least a reliable measure as well as one whose correlates suggest a valid one.[19] 2. Not only are political elites divided on the issues, but where we have comparable data for political elites and the general public, highly educated members of the public are about equally divided and those who are not so highly educated are also divided, but certainly not to the same degree. This does not answer the question about who is leading whom, although it is probably a good assumption that political elites are important in shaping the beliefs of the public.[20] What it does, however, suggest is that the public, especially the most sophisticated part, is not just "sorted," it is divided about to the same degree as the political elites included in the Annenberg survey studies, and these are important elite groups in the American political system. This does not mean that the public is "polarized" in the sense that opinions necessarily cluster at the two extremes of a distribution (strongly "for" or "against" on an issue or question), but it does mean that there are noteworthy differences in the views of conservatives and liberals and that those differences have at least the potential to buttress gridlock in politics, as has been the case in recent years.

Whether one wants to use the term "sorted" or "polarized," it is clear that US politics is increasingly divided along ideological lines, with each political party (particularly the Republicans)[21] increasingly tied to an ideological label. It is also clear that the Congress is increasingly polarized, with a situation now where there is little or no overlap in the ideological positions of Members of the House or even of Senators.[22]

Conclusion

This chapter addressed issues related to polarization and reviewed and analyzed findings from a unique set of surveys that let us compare the general public and several government elite groups. Not surprisingly, given the time of the Annenberg study (2004–2005), conservatives and liberals differed in all of the groups, although they still saw government as having responsibilities (though with markedly different priorities) in areas such as reducing poverty, conserving the country's natural resources and promoting racial equality. And in areas where the differences were most marked, such as taxation, protecting the unborn and promoting stronger morals, the differences are quite great. Further, while as one might expect, the differences were greater among the governmental elites than among the public at large, a simple control for educational level made the gap between conservatives and liberals among the highly educated part of the public mirror the gap between conservatives and liberals among the governmental elites.

One can argue that had the congressional interviews been with Members of Congress or Senators rather than with their staff that the congressional data would have shown greater differences. That is certainly possible, but high-level personal staffers – those interviewed for the Institutions of American Democracy project – are quite likely to reflect the views of their bosses; indeed to be chosen for precisely this reason. In any event, while these data may not definitively settle the matter, there is not much difference between the educated public and the political elites in answering the study questions on responsibilities of the federal government. Both show approximately the same level of difference. So, while the splits and the definitions of the issues of what goes with a conservative or a liberal view may well be led by political elites (and the related media, as well), it appears, at least with respect to the responsibilities of the federal government, that the educated public has either bought it wholesale or been equally moved by the same social and political forces that have reshaped elite politics.

Endnotes

1 The earlier work is in Joel D. Aberbach, "The Future of the American Right: Evidence and Questions from the Bush Years," Joel D. Aberbach and Gillian Peele, eds., *Crisis of Conservatism? The Republican Party, the Conservative Movement, and American Politics after Bush* (New York: Oxford University Press, 2011), pages 40–67.

2 Sean M. Theriault, *Party Polarization in Congress* (Cambridge: Cambridge University Press, 2008), page 8.

3 Theriault, *Polarization* (2008), page 42.

4 For interesting data on the influence of conservative think tanks, see Thomas Medvetz, *Think Tanks in America* (Chicago: University of Chicago Press, 2012), page 238, Table B.4, where Medvetz orders think tanks by their total media citations between 1997 and 2005 and also denotes their political orientations. Of the top ten think tanks in citations, four were designated conservative, three as neutral/centrist and three as liberal. Of the top five, three were conservative (the American Enterprise Institute, the Cato Institute, and the Hoover Institution) and two were neutral/centrist: the Brookings Institution and the Institute for International Economics.

5 Morris P. Fiorina, with Samuel J. Abrams and Jeremy Pope, *Culture War? The Myth of a Polarized America* (New York: Pearson, 2005), page 88.

6 Fiorina et al., *Culture War* (2005), pages 69, 88.

7 The quotation is from Matthew Levendusky, *The Partisan Sort: How Liberals Became Democrats and Conservatives Became Republicans* (Chicago: The University of Chicago Press, 2009), page 132. See also, Morris P. Fiorina and Matthew S. Levendusky, "Disconnected: The Political Class versus the

People," in Pietro S. Nivola and David W. Brady, eds., *Red and Blue Nation? Characteristics and Causes of American's Polarized Politics,* Volume One (Stanford University and Washington: Hoover Institution and Brookings Institution Press, 2006).

8 One example of such an endeavor is M. Kent Jennings, "Ideological Thinking among Mass Publics and Political Elites," *Public Opinion Quarterly,* Vol. 56 (1992), pages 419–441. The study used American National Election Study data and data from surveys of delegates to the 1980 Republican and Democratic national nominating conventions. It found that elites (the delegates) have more constrained political preferences than members of the public including those in the public who reported high engagement in political campaigns.

9 Information on the Annenberg Surveys can be found in Institutions of American Democracy, The Annenberg Democracy Project, *A Republic Divided* (New York: Oxford University Press, 2007), Appendix on the Annenberg Surveys, pages 243–246. Surveys for the project are available online at the Annenberg Public Policy Center web site: http://www.annenbergpublicpolicycenter.org.

10 The question was worded: "In your opinion how important is it for the federal government to do the following? Is (insert) a very important responsibility of the federal government, important, not so important, or not important at all?" The inserted choices were: Conserving the country's natural resources; Keeping taxes low; Protecting the unborn; Promoting stronger morals; Promoting racial equality; and Reducing poverty.

11 The question wording was: "In general, would you describe your views as very conservative, conservative, moderate, liberal, or very liberal?"

12 See Aberbach, "The Future of the American Right" (2011), pages 44–45, for a comparison of the results of answers by the general public to the Annenberg survey version of the ideology question and the American National Election Study (ANES) version.

13 Aberbach, "The Future of the American Right," (2011), page 46.

14 See Joel D. Aberbach and Bert A. Rockman, *In the Web of Politics: Three Decades of the U.S. Federal Executive* (Washington: Brookings Institution Press, 2000), pages 109–114. The results of the Institutions of American Democracy study suggest a top American career bureaucracy that increasingly resembles its European counterparts in its political views (that is, moderate or middle of the road), but that is a subject for another book.

15 Aberbach, "The Future of the American Right" (2011), pages 49–52 and 56–60.

16 See the source note on Figure 6.1.

17 See, especially, pages 227–231, of Philip E. Converse, "The Nature of Belief Systems in Mass Publics," in David Apter, ed., *Ideology and Discontent* (1964), pages 206–261.

18 Zaller compares several indicators of political awareness (including education) and argues that neutral factual information is best, with education and interest as possible supplements. See John R. Zaller, *The Nature and Origins of Mass Opinion* (Cambridge: Cambridge University Press, 1992), pages 335–336. In the Annenberg (Institutions of American Democracy) data the average correlations (gamma) between the ideology measure and the six listed responsibilities of the federal government are .25 for those who did not graduate from college and .44 for those who did.

For a good treatment of the influence of education on political knowledge, see Michael X. Delli Carpini and Scott Keeter, *What Americans Know about Politics and Why It Matters* (New Haven: Yale University Press, 1996), especially pages 182–184 and s77–278.

19 See the discussion of the reliability and validity of this measure in Chapter 2.

20 See Zaller, *The Nature and Origins of Mass Opinion* (1992), pages 98–114, and also page 210 where a general proposition holds that "When elites come to disagree along partisan or ideological lines, the public's response will become ideological as well, with the most politically aware members of the public responding most ideologically."

21 Matt Grossman and David A. Hopkins, "Ideological Republicans and Group Interest Democrats: The Asymmetry of American Party Politics," *Perspectives on Politics*, Vol. 13, No. 1 (March 2015), page 127, Figure 4.

22 See, for example, Gary C. Jacobson, "Partisan Polarization in American Politics: A Background Paper," *Presidential Studies Quarterly*, Vol. 43 (2013), pages 690–694.

7 What Is the Meaning of Contemporary Movements like the Tea Party?[1]

The Tea Party emerged on the scene in 2009, beginning with a rant on the floor of the Chicago Mercantile Exchange by CNBC reporter Rick Santelli who called for a "Chicago Tea Party" to protest government plans to "subsidize the losers' mortgages" as part of its response to the financial crisis of 2008.[2] The reaction across the country was huge, clearly stimulated in part by conservative media and later aided by infusions of funds from major donors, and resulted in the formation of a loosely structured movement whose three main principles, according to a sympathetic analyst, are to promote "limited government," "unapologetic U.S. sovereignty" and "constitutional originalism."[3]

Skocpol and Williamson describe the Tea Party as consisting of "conservative Republican voters." They summarize a 2010 CBS/*New York Times* poll indicating that "the 18 percent of Americans who identify themselves as Tea Party supporters tend to be Republican, white, male, married and older than 45," and say that Tea Party supporters also tend to be "comfortably middle-class" people who "are more likely to be evangelical Protestants than mainline Protestants, Catholics, Jews, or nonbelievers." They are "skeptical, even scornful of 'establishment' Republicans" and are particularly marked by "opposition to public expenditures on education and the environment," while favoring Social Security and Medicare benefits for people like themselves who they deem worthy because they have "earned" them.[4]

At one level, one can see Tea Partiers as an extreme type of contemporary American conservative, but there is more to Tea Partiers than that. They are extraordinarily active in primaries, assisting in the tilt of Republican candidates in their direction, and a recent study by Christopher Parker and Matt Barreto that is likely to be highly controversial argued "that people are driven to support the Tea Party from the anxiety they feel as they perceive the America they know, the country they love, slipping away, threatened by the rapidly changing face of what they believe is the 'real' America: a heterosexual, Christian, middle-class, (mostly) male, white country." Indeed, Parker and Barreto argue, "support for the Tea Party is a proxy for reactionary conservatism."[5]

How reliable the most negative conclusions from the Parker and Barreto study as well as the data on which they are based prove to be cannot be determined fully with the data I have, but they suggest, or so the authors argue, paranoia and status anxiety of the type the historian Richard Hofstadter analyzed in his classic book, *The Paranoid Style in American Politics.*[6] Current indications are that the Tea Party has great influence in Republican politics, but that the often extreme candidates its supporters help nominate tend to repel more moderate conservative voters and that, on balance, the Tea Party phenomenon probably hurts the Republican Party more than it helps.

Who Identifies with the Tea Party?

In keeping with the literature, a simple racial breakdown of the 2012 ANES election survey shows what one would expect (Table 7.1): very few African Americans support the Tea Party. In fact, according to the data in Table 7.1, fewer than 10 percent of African American respondents (8.3 percent to be exact) in the 2012 survey show any degree of support ("strong support," "not very strong support," or "lean toward supporting") for the Tea Party. On the other hand, almost 30 percent of others in the country (28.2 percent) expressed at least some level of support. When it comes to opposition, almost half of African Americans expressed "strong opposition" to the Tea Party, more than double the percentage of non-African Americans (23.1 percent) who expressed the same position ("strong opposition"). So it is fair to say that the Tea Party appeal lies

Table 7.1 Level of Tea Party Support among African Americans Compared to Others in the 2012 ANES Election Survey

Tea Party Support	African Americans	Others
Strong support	4.1	12.8
Not very strong	1.9	7.2
Lean toward supporting	2.3	8.2
Do not lean either way	32.6	39.2
Lean toward opposing	3.3	4.0
Not very strong opposition	8.2	5.3
Strong opposition	47.5	23.1
Total	100.0	100.0

Data Source: 2012 ANES

Question wording:

Tea Party support measure: Do you support, oppose, or neither support nor oppose the Tea Party movement? Would you say that your [support/opposition] is strong or not very strong? If neither: Do you lean toward supporting, lean toward opposing, or do you not lean either way?

mainly outside the African American community, though, as a matter of fact, it is stronger among whites than among any other group. Just a tad over 30 percent of whites express some level of support, compared to 15.6 percent of Hispanics and 23.4 percent of the rest of the population.

Further, men are slightly more likely to support the Tea Party (32.3 percent of non-African American men versus 25.3 percent of non-African American women).[7] As would be expected from the literature, married people are the most likely supporters (35.3 percent), although not by a huge amount (usually about 10 points more than for people with a different marital status) and there was little difference in support by income. Region matters (with more Southerners than Northerners expressing support for the Tea Party) but not all that much. In short, other than a clear non-African American base, Tea Party supporters are not all that distinctive demographically. (*Please note:* From here on in this chapter I will continue the practice of excluding African Americans from the calculations in or to promote comparison to analyses in earlier chapters.)

So who supports the Tea Party? As Table 7.2 shows, liberals of all sorts react very negatively when asked about the Tea Party, and even moderates and those who are slightly conservative are not likely to express support, but about 70 percent of those who identify as conservative or extremely conservative express some level of support (with 56.3 percent of the "Extremely Conservative" expressing strong support and 35.9 percent of the "Conservatives" expressing strong support). Looked at

Table 7.2 Tea Party Support, by Ideology, 2012

Ideology Measure	Percent Supporting Tea Party*
Extremely Liberal	2.8
Liberal	4.6
Slightly Liberal	8.8
Moderate	14.1
Slightly Conservative	32.4
Conservative	68.1
Extremely Conservative	72.4
Gamma	−.63

Data Source: 2012 ANES

Note: African American respondents filtered out.

*Entries are the sum of the percentages expressing "Strong support"; "Not very strong support"; or "Lean toward supporting" the Tea Party.

Question wording:

Tea Party support measure: See Table 7.1.

Ideology measure: Where would you place YOURSELF on this scale, or haven't you thought much about this? Extremely Liberal; Liberal; Slightly Liberal; Moderate; Middle of the Road; Slightly Conservative; Conservative; Extremely Conservative.

Table 7.3 Tea Party Support, by Party ID, 2012

Party ID	Percent Supporting Tea Party*
Strong Democrat	6.1
Not Very Strong Democrat	9.9
Independent Democrat	5.6
Independent	12.9
Independent Republican	52.5
Not Very Strong Republican	38.3
Strong Republican	63.7
Gamma	−.53

Data Source: 2012 ANES
Note: African American respondents filtered out.
*See Table 7.2.

Question wording:

Party ID: Generally speaking, do you usually think of yourself as a [DEMOCRAT, a REPUBLICAN/a REPUBLICAN, a DEMOCRAT], an INDEPENDENT, or what? Would you call yourself a STRONG [Democrat/Republican] or a NOT VERY STRONG Democrat/Republican]? (Recoded to: Strong Democrat; Not Very Strong Democrat; Independent Democrat; Independent; Independent Republican; Not Very Strong Republican; Strong Republican.)

Tea Party support measure: See Table 7.1.

from a different perspective, about 61 percent of the total support of the Tea Party comes from those who say they are conservative or extremely conservative, increasing to 79 percent if one adds in those who say they are slightly conservative. And it is important, further, to keep in mind that Tea Party support, while strongly related to conservative identification, is not at the same level as support for conservatism, at least based on the measures we have. Recall from Chapter 2 that conservative identification hovers just above 40 percent for the non-African American part of the 2012 ANES sample, but Tea Party support for the same population is below 30 percent. The difference is not huge, but it is enough to suggest that there may be at least some subtle differences between the two.

Not surprisingly, given the strong relationship between conservatism and party identification, the same pattern holds for the relationship between party and Tea Party support (Table 7.3) as for ideology and Tea Party support. Here the Tea Party receives 59 percent of its total support from those in the top two categories of Republican identification ("not very strong" and "strong" Republicans), going up to 85 percent of its total support if one adds in "independent" Republicans, where Tea Party support is particularly strong. In fact, it is this strength among people who were classified as independent Republicans that accounts for most of the difference in the correlation coefficients when one compares Tables 7.2 and 7.3, and is one sign of the greater sense of independence that Tea Party people think they represent (as opposed to simple Republican party loyalty). However, as we shall see later in the chapter, in reality Tea Party support was very highly correlated to voting for the Republican Party candidate (Romney) in 2012, and it seems fair to say that supporters of the Tea Party are at their core conservatives who identify with the Republican Party. The "independent" predilection, though, is one sign of their willingness to support challengers to the so-called

Table 7.4 Explaining Tea Party Support, Total and by Education Level, 2012

	Multiple R	*Adjusted R2*
Total	.525	.275
Non-College Graduates	.463	.213
College Graduates	.609	.370

Data Source: 2012 ANES

Note: African American respondents filtered out.

Independent Variables:

- When should abortion be allowed
- Religions service attendance
- Government aid to blacks
- Government guaranteed standards of living

Question Wordings:

Tea Party support measure: See Table 7.1.

Education: What is the highest level of school you have completed or the highest degree you have received?

Abortion: There has been some discussion about abortion during recent years. Which one of the opinions on this page best agrees with your view? You can just tell me the number of the opinion you choose.

1 By law, abortion should never be permitted.
2 The law should permit abortion only in case of rape, incest, or when the woman's life is in danger.
3 The law should permit abortion for reasons other than rape, incest, or danger to the woman.
4 By law, a woman should always be able to obtain an abortion as a matter of personal choice.

Religious Service Attendance: Do you go to religious services [EVERY WEEK, ALMOST EVERY WEEK, ONCE OR TWICE A MONTH, A FEW TIMES A YEAR, or NEVER]?

Note: Variable recoded into five categories:

1) Every week
2) Almost every week
3) Once or twice a month
4) Few times a year
5) Never.

Government Aid to Blacks: Where would you place YOURSELF on this [7pt scale govt assistance to blacks scale] scale, or haven't you thought much about this?

Guaranteed Standards of Living: Where would you place YOURSELF on this [7pt scale guaranteed job-income scale] scale, or haven't you thought much about this?

"Republican establishment" in party primary elections, an important source of Tea Party influence.

Explaining Tea Party Support

Following on from the previous section, the next question is how well the simple model I have been using to explain conservative identification does in explaining Tea Party support. And the short answer (Table 7.4) is that it does quite well. The same set of variables that perform well in the ideology model (see Table 5.6) also, not surprisingly given the clear relationship between conservatism and Tea Party support, are strong predictors of attitudes towards the Tea Party.

The one exception is religious service attendance. While correlated, as expected, with Tea Party support, the zero-order relationship is not as strong as the others and it loses statistical significance when the other variables are taken into account. This is yet another indication that conservatism (in the case of the Tea Party, an endorsement of a contemporary form of conservative activism) and religiosity, while related, are not simply synonymous. Religious service attendance, however, is just one measure of religious commitment, since many people attend religious services for social reasons, and there is certainly a progressive tradition that exists in part of the religious world, depending in part on doctrinal beliefs.[8] To check this out, at least in a preliminary way, I substituted an item measuring a belief that the Bible is the Word of God for the religious service attendance measure as a predictor variable in the multiple regression. That substitution changed the overall result a bit (raising the multiple R from .525 to .548 for the entire sample, and from .463 to .483 for the non-college graduates and from .609 to .636 for college graduates) and produced a statistically significant coefficient for religious belief for the whole group and for both subsamples.

The bottom line, as I said before, is that once one understands the factors contributing to someone expressing strong support for conservatism in surveys of the general public, one is a long way towards understanding who in the public is most likely to endorse the Tea Party, although, to repeat, it is important also to keep in mind that Tea Party support (the percentage of people who support the Tea Party), while strongly correlated with conservative identification, is at a lower level than support for conservatism. (Recall from earlier tables and discussion that over 40 percent of the non-African American part of the sample who answered the question on conservatism expressed some level of conservative identification, whereas only about 28 percent of non-African American respondents indicated any level of support for the Tea Party.)

Let's take a look at a few simple tables.

In Table 7.5, one can see that well more than twice the percentage of people who believe that, by law, abortion should never be permitted support the Tea Party than those who believe that a woman should be able to obtain an abortion as a matter of personal choice (42.1 percent to 16.7 percent). And, more dramatically, in Table 7.6, the relationship between beliefs about the role of government in guaranteeing jobs and a good standard of living for the population (versus those who believe that each person should get ahead on his or her own) is equally strong in correlational terms, but more stunningly visible in percentage terms in the more drawn-out scale used. Here we see that of those who believe that government should ensure jobs and an adequate standard of living for the public, only 11.1 percent express any level of support for the Tea Party. That percentage begins to rise in the middle of the scale and jumps to 62.9 percent for those who believe that each person should get ahead on his or her own. Again, not all who identify with the Tea Party believe this, but the relationship is strong.

One question about Tea Party supporters is tied to their views about race. Skocpol and Williamson cite a 2010 study by Parker et al. to the effect that "problematic racial assumptions are widely held by Tea Party supporters."[9] Indeed, in their book on the Tea Party, Christopher S. Parker and Matt A. Barreto argue that "support for the Tea Party represents a reactionary impulse in which 'Others,' including the president [Obama], are perceived as trying to pry the country away from 'real' Americans." Tea Party supporters, their data suggest, are fearful that minority groups are, in some way, taking their country away, transforming it into something they do not recognize or like. It is, in their terms "a proxy for reactionary conservatism," a conservatism that cannot accept evolutionary change and that is attracted to the type of demagoguery

Table 7.5 Tea Party Support, by Abortion Views, 2012

Abortion Views	Percent Supporting Tea Party*
By law, abortion should never be permitted.	42.1
The law should permit abortion in case of rape, incest or when the women's life is in danger.	38.4
The law should permit abortion for reasons other than rape, incest, or danger to the woman.	31.8
By law, a woman should be able to obtain an abortion as a matter of personal choice.	16.7
Gamma	.38

Data Source: 2012 ANES

Note: African American respondents filtered out.

*See Table 7.2 note.

Question wording:

See Table 7.4 note.

Table 7.6 Tea Party Support by Government Guaranteed Jobs-Income Scale, 2012

Jobs-Income Scale	Percent Supporting Tea Party*
1 Government should see to jobs and standard of living	11.1
2	12.5
3	11.8
4	17.1
5	27.8
6	46.3
7 Government should let each person get ahead on own	62.9
Gamma	−.37

Data Source: 2012 ANES

Note: African American respondents filtered out.

*See Table 7.2 note.

Question wording:

See Table 7.4 note.

"that threatens social order."[10] Skocpol and Williamson, on the other hand, while arguing that the Tea Party is fundamentally the latest iteration of hard-core conservatism in American politics and that the election of Barack Obama inflamed fears that the US is changing in ways they consider undesirable, also emphasize that the negativism of Tea Partiers extends beyond minority groups to anger about those, whites included, who are held back by what Tea Partiers perceive as their own personal failings. As they say: "Tea Partiers rate *whites* [italics in original] relatively poorly on these characteristics, too. Tea Partiers have negative views about all of their fellow citizens; it is just that they make extra-jaundiced assessments of the work ethic of racial and ethnic minorities."[11]

Both of these studies emphasize the social fears that Tea Party adherents hold in our rapidly changing society as well as the focus on President Obama as a threatening and alien force. A subtle difference is that Skocpol and Williamson also stress that the "Tea Party members [they] spoke to were very concerned to assure us that they held no animosity toward black people," an emphasis that at least shows some sensitivity about charges of racism leveled at the movement.[12] But the bottom line is that fears of social change and the perceived threat posed by rising out-groups do seem to mark Tea Party adherents; the question is to what extent compared to others in the society.

While the data I am using do not permit a full answer to this question, they do allow me to look at the racial attitudes of Tea Partiers and their views on some issues that reflect a changing America.

Table 7.7 shows clearly that while the answers to standard questions about race (meaning here African Americans) are strongly related to Tea Party support (as they are to conservatism in general), they are extraordinarily strongly related to questions about the Obama presidency that have racial overtones. This tends to support the contention of Parker and Barreto that race, particularly what they call "Obamaphobia" ("anxiety, fear, and anger" because Obama, to them, represents "tangible evidence that 'their' America is rapidly becoming unrecognizable") is the key to understanding the Tea Party phenomenon in that it is not simply a function of partisanship and commitment to conservatism.[13] However, the picture is somewhat more complicated than that, as we shall now demonstrate.

What makes it more complicated is that those who identify as Tea Party supporters simply very closely resemble in their attitude patterns and behavior those who call themselves conservatives, at least in the ANES data. For example, the correlations between the four variables

Table 7.7 Correlations between Respondents' Beliefs about Race and Tea Party Support, 2012

	Gamma*
1 Tea Party supporters more likely to believe the Obama administration favors blacks over whites.	−.51
2 Tea party supporters more likely to oppose preferential hiring and promotion of blacks.	−.36
3 Tea Party supporters more likely to believe Obama was probably born in another country.	−.55
4 Tea Party supporters more likely to think it's not the government's job to ensure that blacks get fair treatment in jobs.	.38

Data Source: 2012 ANES

Note: African American respondents filtered out.

*Signs of correlations vary according to direction of item answer option. (These correlations are statistically indistinguishable in strength when correlating Respondent's Beliefs about Race with Political Ideology instead of Tea Party Support.) See text.

Question wordings:

Tea Party Support measure: See Table 7.1 note.

Race Administration Favors: Do the policies of the Obama administration favor whites over blacks, favor blacks over whites, or do they treat both groups the same? (Recoded to 1 = Favor Whites; 2 = Equal; 3 = Favor Blacks.)

Preferential Hiring and Promotions: What about your opinion – are you FOR or AGAINST preferential hiring and promotion of blacks?

Obama's Birthplace: Was Barack Obama definitely born in the United States, probably born in the United States, probably born in another country, or definitely born in another country?

Government Ensure Fair Treatment in Jobs: Should the government in Washington see to it that black people get fair treatment in jobs or is this not the federal government's business?

listed in Table 7.7 and Tea Party support are strikingly similar to those
between the same variables and the ideology measure. Three of the four
correlations are almost exactly the same, that is either equal or within .02
of one another – and the one that is most dissimilar (the item on where
President Obama was born), while it might be considered the best test of
"Obamaphobia," is actually very close (the gamma coefficients for the
relationship are –.55 with the Tea Party support item and .49 with the
ideology item, and recall that the signs of the coefficients are different
only because the two variables – Tea Party support and ideology – are
coded in different directions).[14]

 Taking the birth item as a test case because it is the closest to what is
meant by "Obamaphobia," at least in the ANES data, Table 7.8 shows
both the strong similarities and the suggestive differences in the relationships. (Data for the relationship with party identification and ideology
are also in the table for comparative purposes.) First, of course, note
how similar the correlations are. Second, as mentioned in the last paragraph, it is also the case that the Tea Party measure has the largest

Table 7.8 Percent Who Believe President Obama Was Probably or Definitely
Born Abroad, by Tea Party Support, Party ID and Conservatism,
2012

Percent Believing Born Abroad by Tea Party Support		*Percent Believing Born Abroad by Party ID*		*Percent Believing Born Abroad by Ideology*	
Strong support	55.8	Strong Republican	52.3	Extremely Conservative	65.8
Support	42.3	Republican	32.5	Conservative	46.1
Lean toward supporting	37.1	Independent Republican	41.0	Slightly Conservative	25.6
Do not lean either way	26.9	Independent	28.0	Moderate	23.3
Lean toward opposing	19.0	Independent Democrat	8.8	Slightly Liberal	9.4
Oppose	23.0	Democrat	12.7	Liberal	6.2
Strong opposition	4.6	Strong Democrat	7.8	Extremely Liberal	8.7
Gamma*	.55		.48		.49

Data Source: 2012 ANES

Note: African American respondents filtered out.

*Party ID and Ideology measure inverted so that they go in the same direction as Tea Party
Support.

Question wordings:

Obama's Birthplace: See Table 7.7.

Tea Party Support, Party ID, and Ideology measures: See Tables 7.2 and 7.3.

correlation with people's beliefs about where President Obama was born, but, again, the differences are very minor. Third, and most interesting in light of the "Obamaphobia" hypothesis, is that self-identified "extreme conservatives" are even more likely than those who identify as giving "strong support" to the Tea Party to believe that President Obama was probably or definitely born abroad. As an aside, please note that liberals of all stripes reject what it commonly called the "birther" notion about President Obama's place of birth (less than 10 percent of them endorse this notion), while the belief gets the endorsement of about a fifth of those who oppose the Tea Party, but are not in "Strong opposition" (first column on the table).

The conclusion I reach is that Tea Party support and views on race are quite typical of the views of conservatives, especially strongly identified conservatives, and, for that matter, of those who support the contemporary Republican Party. There are some differences, of course, and the belief that President Obama was not born in the United States varies subtly depending on which variable – Tea Party support or ideology or party identification – one uses to predict it, but the similarities are striking. Whether or not the relationship of "Obamaphobia" and Tea Party support (or, for that matter, the other relationships in Table 7.7) are proof of a fairly widespread and deep-seated paranoia in the contemporary US in the style described by the historian Richard Hofstadter is not proven beyond the shadow of a doubt by the type of survey data analyzed here, but it is suggestive.

I'll revisit the theme of the role of race briefly in the concluding chapter, but for now will return the focus to other concerns that apparently motivate Tea Party supporters. These are, for the most part, views that also mark the broader conservative constituency.

First let's look at something as straightforward as the size of government. Respondents were asked whether "ONE, the main reason government has become bigger over the years is because it has gotten involved in things that people should do for themselves, OR: TWO, government has become bigger because the problems we face have become bigger" (ANES, 2012). The relationship between answers to this question and Tea Party Support is (gamma) .59. As Table 7.9a shows, more than 40 percent of the people who think that the government is bigger because it is involved in things people should handle themselves (and that, overall is the position of over 60 percent of the respondents) favor the Tea Party, while only 8 percent of those who think government is bigger because the problems we face are bigger have a favorable view of the Tea Party. Looked at from the perspective of Tea Party support (Table 7.9b), over 90 percent (91.1) of those who strongly support the Tea Party think that the government is bigger because it's involved in things people should handle themselves as compared to 32.4 percent of those who are strongly oppose to the Tea Party.

Table 7.9a Tea Party Support by Views on Government Size, 2012

Views on Why Government Is Bigger	Percent Supporting Tea Party*
Government is bigger because it's involved in things people should handle themselves	42.3
Government is bigger because problems bigger	8.0
Gamma	.59

Data source: 2012 ANES
Note: African American respondents filtered out.
*See Table 7.2 note.
Question wording:
Tea Party support measure: See Table 7.1 note.
Government size: ONE, the main reason government has become bigger over the years is because it has gotten involved in things that people should do for themselves; OR: TWO, government has become bigger because the problems we face have become bigger.

Table 7.9b Government Is Bigger Because It Is Involved in Things People Should Handle Themselves, by Tea Party Support, 2012

Tea Party Support	Percent Agree Government Bigger Because It Is Involved in Things People Should Handle Themselves*
Strong support	91.1
Not very strong	84.6
Lean toward supporting	89.4
Do not lean either way	56.7
Lean toward opposing	52.1
Not very strong opposition	61.0
Strong opposition	32.4
Overall Percent	60.4
Gamma	.59

Data source: 2012 ANES
Note: African American respondents filtered out.
Question wording:
See Table 7.9a.

Not surprisingly, the relationship of the ideology measure and views on why the government is bigger closely resemble those for Tea Party support and explanations for why the government has become bigger (Table 7.9c). By chance, in fact, the correlation is exactly the same as when

Table 7.9c Government Is Bigger Because It Is Involved in Things People Should Handle Themselves, by Ideology, 2012

Ideology	Percent Agree Government Is Bigger Because It Is Involved in Things People Should Handle Themselves
Extremely Liberal	13.5
Liberal	28.2
Slightly Liberal	39.0
Moderate	56.3
Slightly Conservative	72.0
Conservative	87.0
Extremely Conservative	84.8
Overall Percent	60.6
Gamma	−.59

Data source: 2012 ANES

Note: African American respondents filtered out.

Question wording:

See Tables 7.2 and 7.9a notes.

either Tea Party support or ideology is used to predict explanations of why the government is bigger, only with the sign reversed because the measures of conservatism and Tea Party support run in different directions.

When it comes to gun control (**Table 7.10**), we see similar results. More than half of those who want to make it easier for people to get a gun support the Tea Party (57.4 percent) versus only 11.0 percent supporting the Tea Party of those who want to make it more difficult to buy a gun. The same basic relationship holds for the ideology measure (here the gamma coefficient is .44), only, as one might by now guess, those who want to make it more difficult for people to buy a gun tend to be liberals.

Further, and not surprisingly given the results discussed up to now, those who oppose the changing lifestyles that mark modern society also are likely to support the Tea Party. Just take a look at Table 7.11a. Over half of those who agree strongly that newer lifestyles are breaking down society are Tea Party supporters at some level, while fewer than 10 percent of those who disagree strongly with the notion that newer lifestyles are breaking down society support the Tea Party. Looking at this from the perspective of Tea Party support (see Table 7.11b) gives one an even more vivid picture of the relationship (and of the quite widespread support in the US – 59.1 percent in the subsample in this table – for the notion that newer lifestyles are corrosive). Over 80 percent of those who strongly support the Tea Party think newer lifestyles are breaking down society, compared to 31 percent expressing strong opposition to the Tea

Table 7.10 Tea Party Support by Views on Gun Control, 2012

Views on Gun Control	Percent Supporting Tea Party*
Make it more difficult to get a gun	11.0
Keep the rules the same	39.8
Make it easier to get a gun	57.4
Gamma	−.50

Data Source: 2012 ANES

Note: African American respondents filtered out.

*See Table 7.2 note.

Question wording:

Tea Party support measure: See Table 7.1.

Gun Control: Do you think the federal government should make it MORE DIFFICULT for people to buy a gun than it is now, make it EASIER for people to buy a gun, or KEEP THESE RULES ABOUT THE SAME as they are now?

Recoded to: 1) More difficult

　　　　　　2) Keep rules same

　　　　　　3) Easier

Party. And note that endorsement of the proposition about newer lifestyles is the case for more than 50 percent of the respondents who were not strong opponents of the Tea Party.

Table 7.11a Tea Party Support by Newer Lifestyles Breaking Down Society, 2012

Newer Lifestyles Are Breaking Down Society	Percent Supporting Tea Party*
Agree strongly	52.1
Agree somewhat	28.8
Neither agree nor disagree	16.8
Disagree somewhat	14.0
Disagree strongly	8.6
Gamma	.45

Data Source: 2012 ANES

Note: African American respondents filtered out.

*See Table 7.2 note.

Question wording:

Tea Party support measure: See Table 7.1.

New lifestyles breaking down society: 'The newer lifestyles are contributing to the breakdown of our society.' (Do you [AGREE STRONGLY, AGREE SOMEWHAT, NEITHER AGREE NOR DISAGREE, DISAGREE SOMEWHAT, or DISAGREE STRONGLY] with this statement?)

Table 7.11b Newer Lifestyles Are Breaking Down Society, by Tea Party Support, 2012

Tea Party Support	Percent Agree Strongly or Somewhat That Newer Lifestyles Are Breaking Down Society*
Strong support	84.0
Not very strong	82.7
Lean toward supporting	72.5
Do not lean either way	60.1
Lean toward opposing	50.8
Not very strong opposition	66.9
Strong opposition	31.3
Overall percent saying newer lifestyles are breaking down society	59.1
Gamma	.45

Data Source: 2012 ANES

Note: African American respondents filtered out.

*Percent is total of "agree strongly" or "agree somewhat" that newer lifestyles are breaking down society.

<u>Question wording</u>:
See Table 7.11.

Without belaboring the point too much further, we can see from Table 7.11c that it is the liberals (a distinct minority of the sample in percentage terms as compared to the more robust percentages who identify as some level of conservative or as moderate) who are the holdouts against the notion that newer lifestyles are contributing to the breakdown of US society, though with even those who are "slightly liberal" cross the 40 percent threshold in supporting the notion that newer lifestyles are breaking down society.

Are the Tea Party Supporters Operational Liberals?

So now we come to an intriguing question, at least in terms of the literature: Are the Tea Party supporters operational liberals or, at minimum, are they operational liberals in areas that affect them directly? Certainly, some writers have emphasized that "national groups [linked to the Tea Party] endeavor to keep 'Tea Party' aims vague and general [because] 'eliminating the deficit' sounds fine to regular citizens, but specifics such as the abolition of Medicare are not popular at the grass roots, even with Tea Party people."[15] It would not be surprising, then, for Tea Party supporters to distinguish between government benefits they have "earned,"

Table 7.11c Newer Lifestyles Are Breaking Down Society, by Ideology, 2012

Ideology	Percent Agree Strongly or Somewhat That Newer Lifestyles Are Breaking Down Society*
Extremely Liberal	19.7
Liberal	25.4
Slightly Liberal	41.8
Moderate	55.2
Slightly Conservative	68.3
Conservative	84.9
Extremely Conservative	83.1
Overall percent saying newer lifestyles are breaking down society	59.2
Gamma	−.49

Data Source: 2012 ANES

Note: African American respondents filtered out.

*Percent is total of "agree strongly" or "agree somewhat" that newer lifestyles are breaking down society.

<u>Question wording</u>:
See Tables 7.2 and 7.11.

like Social Security or Medicare, and those that budget-busting "free-loaders" receive like welfare.

Table 7.12 is a table of correlations between the variable measuring support for the Tea Party and views on whether federal spending in a variety of areas should be increased, remain the same, or decreased. (*Please note:* Because the Tea Party measure runs from Strong Support (1) to Strong Opposition (7), and the Federal Spending measures go from Increase (1) to Decrease (3), a negative correlation indicates that Tea Party supporters are the most likely to favor deceases in expenditures.) What the table shows is that support for the Tea Party is, indeed, correlated very weakly or not at all with views on spending on Social Security (weakly) or on programs dealing with crime (not at all), but that there are some moderate (spending on science and technology or on aid to public education) to strong (for example, spending on welfare or on the environment) negative relationships indicating that Tea Party supporters are less likely than others to favor increased spending in these areas and, as a matter of fact, more likely than Tea Party opponents to favor decreased spending levels. Indeed, Tea Party supporters, like conservatives in general, show clear signs that they are more likely than other citizens to favor decreased spending in many areas identified with liberalism.

Table 7.12 Are Tea Partiers Operational Liberals? Tea Party Support and Views on Federal Spending, 2012

	Gamma*
Spending on science and technology	−.27
Spending on Social Security	−.11
Spending on aid to public education	−.27
Spending on dealing with crime	.01
Spending on welfare	−.41
Spending on the environment	−.49
Spending on aid to the poor	−.36
Spending on child care	−.37

Data Source: 2012 ANES

Note: African American respondents filtered out.

*Entries are Gamma coefficients of the relationship between the Tea Party Support measure and views on spending in the listed areas. A negative coefficient indicates that Tea Party supporters are the most likely to favor decreases in expenditures.

Question Wordings:

Tea Party support measure: See Table 7.1 note.

All questions for federal spending areas: Should federal spending on [federal program/issue area] be INCREASED, DECREASED, or kept ABOUT THE SAME?

[Wordings of federal programs and issue areas are as stated in table.]

Note: All recoded to:

1 = Increased

2 = Kept the same

3 = Decreased; Cut out entirely.

However, and this is the key, the data also show that many Tea Party supporters favor spending in these areas, just not to the same extent as others. Take spending on the poor for example, where the correlation between Tea Party support and support for federal spending is −.36; what the data show is that while almost half (48 percent) of strong Tea Party supporters favor decreasing spending in this area, this drops into the 30s for less strong supporters and below 10 percent (8.1 percent to be exact) for strong opponents of the Tea Party. So the relationship is quite pronounced, but the overall percentage favoring either increased spending or keeping expenditures for aiding the poor at the current level (the larger category among all Tea Party supporters) is 68 percent. When one uses the word welfare, however, a term often conflated with race because of the perception that African Americans are the main recipients of welfare (though, as noted in Chapter 4, African Americans are not the majority of those on welfare,[16] the percentages of Tea Party supporters (and others) who favor decreased spending shoot up, a finding in line with the racial attitudes of many Tea Party respondents. Almost

80 percent (78.6) of strong Tea Party supporters favor decreased federal spending on welfare, and over 70 percent of other Tea Party supporters feel the same way. The percent favoring decreased spending drops below 50 percent after that, but not by much – it is about 47 percent for those who do not lean one way or another on the Tea Party and those who lean towards opposing or do not express strong opposition. It is only among those who strongly oppose the Tea Party that support for decreased federal spending on welfare drops below 30 percent (28.7).

The bottom line is that Tea Party supporters, like other conservatives (and they are more often than not one and the same), tend to support decreases in federal spending in many areas more than those who express opposition to the Tea Party, and that when it comes to particularly controversial spending areas that are tinged with race, such as welfare, the "operational liberal" label clearly does not fit. However, overall, Tea Party supporters oppose decreases in many federal programs beyond Social Security. (And on Social Security, only 11.4 percent want to see a decrease, while 34.7 percent want to see an increase in spending.) Even in an area like federal spending on child care, more Tea Party supporters favor either increases or, especially, level funding, rather than decreases.

How Important Are Tea Party Supporters in Presidential Politics?

One of the more interesting things about Tea Party adherents is said to be their import in electoral politics, and most especially in the citizen participation side of nominating politics. Tea Party favorites have won upset victories in primaries and have then gone on to general election contests, sometimes to victories and at other times to defeats that have cost the Republican Party greatly.[17]

Looking first at voting in presidential elections (Table 7.13), it is no surprise that Tea Party supporters voted for the Republican candidate (Romney) in 2012. And it is also no surprise that the stronger one's support for the Tea Party, the greater the percentage who voted for Romney, although the differences are not great, going from 87.7 percent for Romney among those who "lean toward supporting" the Tea Party to 94.4 percent of those who strongly support the Tea Party. Even those who do not lean either way tended to support Romney, while those who expressed "strong opposition" were overwhelmingly likely to vote for the Democratic candidate (Obama).

So how does this compare to support for Romney based on scores on the ideology (liberal/conservative) measure? What's stunning is how similar the findings are, especially at the conservative end of the spectrum. Not only is the correlation between the ideology and vote variables almost exactly the same (gamma = .86, with the sign difference a function of the direction of the coding of the ideology variable – from "Extremely

Table 7.13 General Election Vote for Romney, by Tea Party Support, 2012

Tea Party Support	Percent Voting for Romney
Strong support	94.4
Not very strong	91.4
Lean toward supporting	87.7
Do not lean either way	53.1
Lean toward opposing	47.8
Not very strong opposition	47.5
Strong opposition	8.7
Gamma	−.81

Data Source: 2012 ANES

Note: African American respondents filtered out.

Question wording:

Tea Party support measure: See Table 7.1 note.

2012 general election vote: Who did you vote for? Barack Obama, Mitt Romney/Mitt Romney, Barack Obama, or someone else?

Liberal" to "Extremely Conservative"), but 94.9 percent of "Extremely Conservative" identifiers reported voting for Romney, almost exactly the same as the percentage of those who expressed "strong support" for the Tea Party (94.4 percent). Those who identified as "Conservative," but not as "Extremely Conservative," also voted overwhelmingly for Romney, especially the large number of voters simply scored as "Conservative," who voted 94.5 percent for Romney. Once again it is the liberals of all stripes who are on the other side, with more than 95 percent reporting a vote for Obama. The major difference between the two variables (ideology and Tea Party support) on vote is among "Moderates" on ideology where Obama received a majority (as opposed to the majority for Romney among those who do not lean either way on the Tea Party).

Turning to primary voting and party caucus attendance, it is here that Tea Party supporters stand out. Table 7.14 breaks down presidential primary voting for those who identify as Republican by their level of support for the Tea Party. What one sees immediately is how much larger the percentage is of strong supporters of the Tea Party who voted in primaries or attended a party caucus than is the case for those who lean toward supporting the Tea Party or, especially, do not have a position on the Tea Party or oppose it. Over half of the strong supporters and even of the not very strong supporters of the Tea Party who identified as Republicans participated in the nominating process, and participation dropped off quite a bit after that.

Table 7.14 Percent Voted in Presidential Primary or Caucus, by Tea Party
Support, Republican Identifiers Only,* 2012

Tea Party Support	Percent Voted in Presidential Primary or Caucus, Republican Identifiers Only
Strong support	58.2
Not very strong	54.2
Lean toward supporting	41.9
Do not lean either way	32.0
Lean toward opposing	32.1
Not very strong opposition	29.4
Strong opposition	35.3
Overall Percent	42.9
Gamma	.31

Data Source: 2012 ANES

Note: African American respondents filtered out.

*Republican identifiers include Independent Republicans, Not Very Strong Republicans, and Strong Republicans.

Question wording:

Tea Party support measure: See Table 7.1 note.

2012 primary or caucus vote: Did you vote in a Presidential primary election or caucus this year?

Comparing the results of Table 7.14 to a similar analysis using the ideology measure as the independent variable yields the easily predictable similar results (see Table 7.15). Among Republican Party identifiers, "Extremely Conservative" respondents were the most likely to participate in primaries or caucuses (61.6 percent) and the figures dropped off considerably (to the mid-30 percent or lower range) for the modest number of liberal or middle of the road Republican identifiers. Perhaps most telling, "Slightly Conservative" respondents also participate in Republican primaries or caucuses at a modest level (35.4 percent) compared to their more conservative brethren. This is comparable to the finding for those who "lean toward supporting" the Tea Party (Table 7.13) where primary or caucus participation is relatively low.

The bottom line is clear. Tea Party supporters, especially those who are the most supportive of the Tea Party movement, are major players in the public part of the Republican nominating process. To a large extent, these figures mirror the influence of those who identify as conservatives, especially strong conservatives, because they are, by and large, an overlapping set of people. (Over 80 percent of the strong

Table 7.15 Percent Voted in Presidential Primary or Caucus, by Ideology, Republican Identifiers Only,* 2012

Ideology	Percent Voted in Presidential Primary or Caucus, Republican Identifiers Only
Extremely Liberal	**
Liberal	**
Slightly Liberal	35.0
Moderate	32.8
Slightly Conservative	35.4
Conservative	52.6
Extremely Conservative	61.6
Overall Percent	43.9
Gamma	−.31

Data Source: 2012 ANES

Note: African American respondents filtered out.

*Republican identifiers include Independent Republicans, Not Very Strong Republicans, and Strong Republicans.

**Fewer than 25 respondents.

Question wording:

Ideology measure: See Table 7.2.

2012 primary or caucus vote: Did you vote in a Presidential primary election or caucus this year?

Tea Party supporters who participated in Republican primaries or caucuses, for example, identified as either "Conservative" or "Extremely Conservative.") Republican elected officials generally pay a lot of attention to these folks because they have relatively little choice, and those whose candidacies depend on primaries or caucuses (which is most of them) are at minimum torn between what are often the broader views of their constituencies and the views of those who play a disproportionate role in selecting them to run for office.

Conclusion

The Tea Party phenomenon, born in 2009, has been a potent force in American politics. The data analyzed in this chapter indicate that support for the Tea Party and the views of Tea Partiers resemble the comparable data for those who identify as conservatives, and this should not be a surprise given the significant overlap between the two.[18] Whether Tea Party supporters are the paranoid types suggested by Parker and Barreto on the basis of their data[19] is not something I can establish with the ANES survey results, but Tea Party supporters, like many others who identify as conservatives in the contemporary US, tend to be socially traditional, distressed about newer lifestyles and trends in modern society, and slightly more than half of strong supporters of the Tea Party, even after President Obama's release of his birth certificate in 2011, still believed that he was definitely or probably born abroad. In fact, the data indicate that many Tea Party backers, like others who identify as "Conservative" or "Extremely Conservative," have quite negative views on issues connected to race, and this despite the efforts of some of their leaders to dispel the notion that race plays an important role in Tea Party support. Finally, Tea Party backers, like the strong conservatives with whom they overlap, are very active in Republican primaries, a factor that clearly contributes to their level of influence over Republican office holders.

Endnotes

1 The introduction to this chapter is reproduced, with some minor modifications, from Joel D. Aberbach, "Understanding American Political Conservatism," published in Robert Scott and Stephen Kosslyn, eds., *Emerging Trends in the Social and Behavioral Sciences* (Hoboken, NJ: John Wiley and Sons, 2015).

2 Quoted in Theda Skocpol and Vanessa Williamson, *The Tea Party and the Remaking of Republican Conservatism* (New York: Oxford University Press, 2012), page 7.

3 Elizabeth Price Foley, *The Tea Party* (New York: Cambridge University Press, 2012), page 19. On the backing of the Tea Party, see Skocpol and Williamson, *The Tea Party and the Making of American Conservatism,* pages 9–10; and Kate Zernike, *Boiling Mad* (New York : Times Books, 2010), page 43.

4 The quoted material in this paragraph is from Skocpol and Williamson, *The Tea Party and the Remaking of Republican Conservatism* (2012), pages 147, 23 (citing a *New York Times*/CBS News Poll and a Pew Research Center report), pages 27, 28, and 60–61.

5 Christopher S. Parker and Matt A. Barreto, *Change They Can't Believe In: The Tea Party and Reactionary Politics in America* (Princeton: Princeton University Press, 2013), pages 3 and 244.

6 See Richard Hofstadter, *The Paranoid Style in American Politics* (New York: Vintage Books, 1967).

7 African American respondents were filtered out in this calculation as in all future calculations in this chapter, mainly, as before, because of the strong tendency toward uniform political affiliation and voting choice among African Americans.

8 See Ryan L. Claassen, *Godless Democrats and Pious Republicans? Party Activists, Party Capture, and the "God Gap"* (New York: Cambridge University Press, 2015), pages 141–146 on traditionalism (orthodoxy in religion) and tradition (attendance at religious services, the most common measure used in religious studies). There is a strong relationship between the two in the 2012 ANES data; gamma = .57.

9 Skocpol and Williamson, *The Tea Party and the Remaking of Republican Conservatism* (2012), page 69.

10 The quotations are from Parker and Barreto, *Change They Can't Believe In* (2013), pages 156, 244, and 40–43.

11 Skocpol and Williamson, *The Tea Party and the Remaking of Republican Conservatism* (2012), page 69. Also see page 82.

12 Skocpol and Williamson, *The Tea Party and the Remaking of Republican Conservatism* (2012), page 69.

13 Parker and Barreto, *Change They Can't Believe In* (2013), pages 191 and 192.

14 Other correlations with the variables listed in the table and the ideology (liberal/conservative) measure are .52 with the administration favors blacks over whites, .36 with opinion on preferential hiring of blacks and −.38 on whether the government should provide fair treatment in jobs for blacks. Recall that the way the Tea Party and ideology measures are coded accounts for the sign differences on the coefficients.

15 Skocpol and Williamson, *The Tea Party and the Remaking of Republican Conservatism* (2012), page 110.

16 Martin Gilens, *Why Americans Hate Welfare* (Chicago: University of Chicago Press, 1999), Chapter 5, especially page 107.

17 In a highly publicized, though unusual case, Christine O'Donnell, a Tea Party activist, defeated former Delaware governor Michael Castle in the Republican primary to determine the party's Senate nominee in 2010, but lost the election in a swirl of controversy about witchcraft. See Frank Bruni, "With O'Donnell as Foil, Democrat Plays It Safe," *New York Times,* October 11, 2010. Other controversies, especially over abortion rights, have plagued Tea Party candidates in general elections.

18 If ideology and Party ID are regressed on the Tea Party support variable, both are significant but the ideology variable has a higher beta.

19 Parker and Barreto, *Change They Can't Believe In* (2013), page 242.

8   Varieties of Conservatism
Comparative and Domestic Perspectives

This chapter looks at some important aspects of conservatism in comparative perspective. The first section focuses on a comparison of United States and United Kingdom conservatism, with emphasis on why the UK Conservative Party has modified and moderated its message while the Republican Party in the US has struggled relatively unsuccessfully with the same issues. The second section briefly lays out the varieties of conservatism among US conservative elites, an area that often divides the activists in the movement.

UK and US Conservatism: Some Comparisons

The UK: The UK Conservative Party, led by Margaret Thatcher for most of the period, was in power from 1979 to 1997. (Mrs. Thatcher was Prime Minister from 1979 to 1990. John Major, her successor, held the office from her ousting/resignation as Conservative Party leader in 1990 to 1997.) This long period, certainly successful in electoral terms, was also a time when the party had a distinctive ideological bent (neo-liberalism), and, as such, gives us a chance to look at some of the circumstances under which a conservative party might adjust its basic message since the party then went through a 13-year electoral drought before coming back into office (in coalition with the smaller Liberal Democrat Party after the 2010 election.

Mrs. Thatcher was an unusual leader of the Conservative Party, and not merely because she was the first female leader. Her party was long noted for its ability to adapt and to win elections. It was the heir to the conservatism of Edmund Burke and as such was a pragmatic, office-seeking party that had adapted, though often without great enthusiasm, to the changes in its environment. It was a party where "flexibility in the face of change was trumpeted as the key to [its] electoral success." Indeed, Hayton noted, a notion popular among Conservatives was that "theirs was a non-ideological party.[1] As Nigel F. B. Allington and Gillian Peele wrote in 2012: "Traditionally the Conservative Party has been seen as an organization which valued unity and loyalty above ideology or policy division . . . Yet the period from Thatcher's victory in 1975 as Leader of the Opposition after the 1974 general election defeat of Conservative Prime Minister Edward Heath until today has seen an unusual degree of often damaging internal division."[2] Rejecting the "One Nation Conservatism" that marked many of her predecessors, a conservatism that focused on inclusive rhetoric and on policies that accepted the basic welfare reforms put into place to ameliorate the effects of the industrial revolution on the working-class population (often called Butskellism after the relatively similar policies of the Conservatives and Labour Parties identified with R. A. (Rab) Butler and Hugh Gaitskell in the wake of World War II), Mrs. Thatcher espoused a strong neo-liberal philosophy that put great emphasis on the role of markets, the regulation of Britain's powerful trade unions and "most dramatically of all, the privatization of many of the industries which had been in public ownership since the Labour administration of Clement Attlee after 1945."[3]

These policies, combined with her outspoken endorsement of a theoretical position that, in accord with the market philosophy of neo-liberalism, put great emphasis on the individual rather than society in essence made Mrs. Thatcher a theorist in a conservative party that had its roots in the anti-theoretical – adaptation through the wisdom of experience – world of traditional conservatism. She famously said:

> And, you know, there's no such thing as society. There are individual men and women, and there are families. And no government can do anything except through people, and people must look after themselves first.[4]

The contrast of this statement to one made by Harold Macmillan, a revered former Conservative Prime Minister (1957 to 1963), in his maiden speech to the House of Lords during the divisive coal miners' strike of 1984 that broke the power of their union says it all about the difference between the One Nation types and the Thatcherites:

> It breaks my heart to see . . . what is happening in our country today. This terrible strike, by the best men in the world, who beat the Kaiser's and Hitler's armies and never gave in. It is pointless and we cannot afford that kind of thing.
>
> Then there is the growing division of comparative prosperity in the south and an ailing north and Midlands. We used to have battles and rows, but they were quarrels. Now there is a new kind of wicked hatred that has been brought in by different kinds of people.[5]

The coal miners' strike was only one of many conflicts during the Thatcher period. Her many triumphs, including victory in the Falklands War and her economic policies, made her a symbol of British resurgence to some, especially in her own party and abroad, and of what came to be called the "Nasty Party" by others. Mrs. Thatcher was eventually brought down in a leadership challenge in 1990 (her government had grown increasingly unpopular and an election was nearing) and succeeded by John Major who led the Conservatives to victory in 1992, and then to defeat by a resurgent "New Labour" party in 1997. Labour then governed for the next 13 years before its defeat in 2010 by the David Cameron-led Conservatives and its eventual coalition partner, the Liberal Democrats.

The defeat of the Major government was likely in part a reaction to its handling of Britain's withdrawal from the European Exchange Rate Mechanism following the 1992 election and to scandals that dogged the party, but it was also a reflection of a change in the Labour Party under Tony Blair. Labour shed its image as a party dominated by what to many were outdated and counterproductive socialist and union-dominated policies and, one could argue, espoused a form of neo-liberalism with a more human face. Whatever one thinks of the approach, the Labour Party made a wrenching adjustment and secured victory. Why did the Conservatives, who were known for their dedication to electoral victory, fail to do the same for much of the period following the 1997 defeat? That is the question, and it has been a subject of intense analysis by British political scientists as well as journalists and others.

Perhaps the major work on the subject is by Tim Bale, reported in his book on *The Conservative Party: From Thatcher to Cameron*. He describes the task of his book as "not so much to explain why the Conservative Party lost elections," [rather] "to explain why those politicians [in the party] were unwilling and unable to act in a way that might have given them more hope of winning or at least losing less badly."[6]

Bale argues that the Conservatives went for many years defying the assumption that they would make fundamental changes because, despite defeat, parties are more than just machines to win elections. They are heavily influenced by activists, donors, media supporters, and, in the Tory (Conservative) case in this period, by the substantial number of Thatcherites among the party's Parliamentary membership. In fact, he says, unlike Labour after the disastrous defeat it suffered when led by the very left-wing Michael Foot in the 1983 general election, the Tories "made only the most half-hearted attempts or no attempts at all" to "manoeuvre their party back into the mainstream." They didn't change all that much because the core people who were in the party and those who supported them didn't want to change in significant ways. Their leaders attempted to make changes, but failed for the most part, and, argues Bale, William Hague, the leader from 1997 to 2001 rejected change because he thought that previous efforts had proven "fruitless."[7]

Finally, the party turned to David Cameron who assumed the leadership position at a time when the party was, Bale writes, both "more malleable and more manageable than the one with which his predecessors were confronted." The argument is that by 2005, the year Cameron became leader, the influence of Mrs. Thatcher had waned (in fact, about half of the Conservative Members of Parliament at that time were initially elected post-Thatcher), and the members had developed a "hunger" for victory, and that included even most of the right-wing media. This gave Cameron the room to talk change and to celebrate an image of the Tories as committed to building what he called the "Big Society." Bale provides a classic Cameron quote: "Yes, we're the party of strong borders, law and order and low taxes, and we always will be. But today we're also the party of the NHS [National Health Service], the environment, and of social justice too." Or, as Bale so charmingly puts it: "Ideology was out, and pragmatism was in."[8]

There are other analyses of Cameron's words and actions that, while perhaps more cynical, are not necessarily incompatible with the underlying message of the Bale book. For example, Richard Hayton concludes his book, cited earlier in the chapter, and titled *Reconstructing Conservatism? The Conservative Party in Opposition, 1997–2010*, with some skepticism about whether Cameron represents a return to the Conservative Party's grand days of the One Nation tradition. He sees the negotiation of the coalition government deal with the Liberal Democrats as a pragmatic attempt to convince them that the Conservatives had "changed sufficiently" to justify an agreement and he believes that Cameron's reconstruction of the party, while "a long and difficult process" has been "fundamentally limited in scope." And he disagrees with those who see Cameron as a "One Nation Conservative" and certainly not, as one Conservative MP put it, the "heir to Disraeli." His main criticism is that "Cameron steered his party within rather than against Thatcherism's wake," and that "Cameron succeeded in presenting a fresh face of modern conservatism, but that this was in large part a case of rebranding and repackaging a neo-Thatcherite product, rather than re-orienting the ideological trajectory of his party."[9]

I think it fair to say that UK budgets under PM Cameron have been tough and that his general approach to the economy is in the neo-liberal tradition, but his rhetoric (the "Big Society," for example)[10] and efforts in the social policy area are far from the Thatcherite view which rejects the notion that there is such a thing as society. And the fact that Cameron has negotiated his way through a difficult policy thicket in a way that causes some questions about where his commitments lie can be seen as a piece in the pragmatic tradition that has marked British conservatism over the years. In that sense, he has succeeded where his predecessors failed. The rebranding Hayton talks about is not simply fluff, but is based on a set of changes such as the party-splitting gay marriage bill in 2013[11] that have, at least to the 2015 election, made the Conservative Party more attractive (and certainly less threatening) to the moderate part of the electorate and better able than it was before to sustain itself in a difficult electoral environment. However, because the rhetoric may well outrun the reality, one must suspend judgment, especially in the area of public spending on social benefits.[12]

In the end, the party came back from its long electoral slump by successfully modifying its message, doing some things to back up its new claims, and generally communicating a return to the underlying One Nation perspective that has kept the Conservative Party viable through generations of moderate change in the Burkean tradition. The necessity to follow this path in order to get the party back in control of Parliament evidently overcame the deeply committed neo-liberal insurgency that dominated through the Thatcher years and for many years thereafter until it was whittled down by a combination of defeat, clever marketing, and some actual changes as well.

As Hayton writes, "David Cameron was more successful than his three predecessors in consistently pursuing a message of change and modernization of the party, and presenting it credibly. His major advantage in this regard was that after three heavy electoral defeats both the parliamentary party and the wider membership were more easily persuadable of the importance of changing its image messages and strategy."[13]

How that all compares to the course of the contemporary counterpart to the Conservative Party in the United States, the Republican Party, is significant for understanding conservative politics in the US.

The US: Chapter 6 summarized the academic debate about political polarization in the United States. Whatever one's view about whether the political divisions in the country should be described as polarized or sorted, there is little doubt that there is now a deep party division in the Congress and among the political, intellectual and parts of the media elite. And as is demonstrated so clearly in Chapters 2, the voters are also now similarly split into parties that are strongly associated with how people place themselves on a scale running from extremely liberal to extremely conservative.

Further, unlike the UK, the Republican Party, the party of most US conservatives, has not for the most part calibrated its positions (moderated) in an attempt to win over the median voter, as at least some might have expected. The questions are why, and with what consequences.

A first obvious question is whether it is fair to focus on the Republicans here. Recent studies suggest that it is. Nolan McCarty, Keith Poole and Howard Rosenthal, for example, analyzing votes in Congress, find that Republicans there are increasingly conservative and that the increase in polarization in Congress is mainly a function of rightward movement by Republicans.[14] Or, to take another example, Matt Grossman and David A. Hopkins find what they call an "asymmetry" between Republicans and Democrats both in the general public and among activists and donors. Basically, they argue: "The Republican Party is primarily the agent of an ideological movement whose supporters prize doctrinal purity, while the Democratic Party is better understood as a coalition of social groups seeking concrete action."[15]

The Grossman and Hopkins statement may exaggerate the difference some, but it fits with the argument of two close observers of Congress, Thomas Mann and Norman Ornstein. Their book titled *It's Even Worse than It Looks* (Basic Books, 2012) is summarized in an even more provocatively titled *Washington Post* op ed. piece titled "Let's Just Say It: The Republicans Are the Problem." There they argue that the moderates in the Republican Party are disappearing from Congress, saying (using the football terminology so beloved by Americans) that "while the Democrats may have moved from their 40-yard line to their 25, the Republicans have gone from their 40 to somewhere behind their goal post."[16]

A second question is whether or not it is rational for the Republicans, the party of the conservatives, to hold so steadfastly to their positions. One possible answer can be found in the data used for this book and in other recent work by academics. Chapter 2 discussed the growing link between party identification and ideology in the general public. It also showed that the public is much more likely to identify with the conservative than the liberal label. What it did not focus on was the fact that of the one-third or so of the general public who when asked about their ideology says that they are moderates, more identified as Democrats (43 percent) than Republicans (33 percent). Therefore, the Democrats partially make up for the fact that they are the party of those who identify as liberals by garnering more support from self-proclaimed moderates than the Republicans receive. This makes one wonder about the narrowly defined political wisdom of the apparent Republican strategy. So, why do they do it?

The answer is that a complex of forces pushes them in this direction. First of all, Republican/conservative activists are highly mobilized (and increasingly so over time) and they, along with a very wealthy set of donors have huge influence over who is nominated to Congress and, consequently, who is elected. Second, as the data in Chapter 7 indicate, the most conservative people among Republicans are the most likely to vote in primaries or attend caucuses. Third, and related closely to point 2, the Tea Party movement within the Republican Party provides a further push towards conservatism by supporting conservative candidates and vilifying non-conservatives. Fourth, there is a strong network of conservative think tanks and, especially, conservative media that provide steady reinforcement to both conservative candidates and strong messages to the part of the attentive general public, particularly those who watch such networks as Fox News or who listen to conservative talk radio.

But beyond this, let us consider comparatively some differences between the UK and the US situations when it comes to conservatism. First, the power of party leaders is much greater in the UK. They have much more say over nominations than the system in the US where primaries now put a huge amount of influence over nominations, relative to party leaders, into the hands of activists and donors. Second, the roles of minorities in the two polities differ. In the US, the African American minority in particular is tightly joined to the Democratic Party. In the UK, the minority vote is much more up for grabs.[17] (One could say that the latter is true in the US with respect to Hispanic voters, but many Republican activists and particularly those seeking nominations for office have frustrated the National Party Committee leaders by making virulently negative remarks about Hispanic immigrants.) Third, there are large numbers of religious people in the US who identify with conservatism and the Republican Party, while the numbers of such people in the UK is quite limited.[18] This gives party leaders greater flexibility because the influence of religious figures is more modest in the UK than in the US. Fourth, the biggest movement of conservative dissenters in the US (the Tea Party) is firmly, though informally, housed within the Republican Party, while in the UK many of those who might be extreme activists on immigration within the Conservative Party are more attracted to the United Kingdom Independence Party (UKIP). Fifth is that Republican politicians often are at one in their beliefs with those in the public who call themselves conservatives (indeed, often with those who are the most strongly identified) and, as Bale notes in his study of the Conservative Party in the UK, "selective perception" may even lead such politicians to see their backers as more right-wing than they actually are,[19] a phenomenon probably magnified in the US because of the huge import of conservatives who are motivated enough to communicate their views and provide funds to the party.

Finally, I put great emphasis on structural factors that differ between the UK and the US. David Cameron became party leader after a string of defeats that left Conservative members of parliament and conservative party adherents in the country hungry for office. They were so anxious for conservatives to take office that they backed a coalition with the Liberal Democrats to secure office in 2010 when the election results necessitated a coalition partner and would do so again were that the price of retaining power.[20] They may not have liked the idea of a coalition, but they preferred that to being in the opposition. In a unified system like the UK's, a party is either in government or in the opposition. Even in coalition, and especially in a coalition that is dominated by the party winning the most votes and the most seats, the big winners are almost always clear because they get more of the cabinet posts and the Prime Minister's office. The losers, in this case Labour, also know that they have lost.

In the American system of separated institutions sharing powers, on the other hand, the losers of the presidential election of course know that they have lost – except sometimes, such as in 2000 when it took a Supreme Court decision to make George Bush president – but they may triumph in the elections deciding control of the House of Representatives or the Senate. For the rough equivalent in the US of the Members of Parliament, the Representatives and Senators, then, an election defeat in the presidential contest may not look all that devastating and a win in the off-year elections may look like a particularly great triumph. In such a system, there is much less incentive for office holders to compromise simply because their party may fail to win the big prize – the presidency. And in the US system – where the votes of the Democrats tend to be concentrated in urban areas, districts are subject to various types of gerrymanders by Republican-controlled state legislatures, and the realignment of the South into a reliably Republican area gives conservatives a good chance to win control of one or both houses of Congress – conservatives may see relatively little reason to change and, in fact, have little reason to see their views as requiring some adjustments in order to gain power. Particularly among the Republicans, who have the large conservative base to rely on, party leaders may plead for moderation, especially among presidential aspirants, but the candidates and the activists who play a big role in nominating them have relatively little incentive to conform. The irony is that the US separation of powers system, meant to promote compromise and accommodation, may, under the conditions like those found in the US today, actually exacerbate conflict. With the conservative southern Democrats a feature of the past (and good riddance to the racist policies they espoused) the architects of compromise are fewer than before.

Varieties of US Conservatives[21]

For most of the book, I have been concerned with understanding the meaning of conservatism to members of the general public. So far in this chapter, the aim has been to get a better perspective on conservatism through a comparison of conservative politics in the United States and the United Kingdom. The view has been broad, focusing mainly on elite politics and why the major policies have or have not adjusted their messages in light of their electoral fortunes. This section looks very briefly at another aspect of elite conservative politics in the United States – the many factions or approaches to conservatism. It is not meant to be a complete guide; rather it is a simplified tour across a complex terrain and hopefully will make some of the issues discussed in the concluding chapter more meaningful.

Chapter 1 discussed *traditional* (Burkean-derived) *conservatism*. This is a conservatism that aims to preserve what is best based on human experience, to make changes when necessary (even if reluctantly), and in general to respect institutions and practices that have evolved over time. It eschews large theoretical propositions in favor of a wisdom that grows out of practice. It focuses on the integrity of the community, the role of religion as part of the foundation of society (though conservatives of this stripe are not necessarily religious themselves), and like the One Nation Conservatives of the UK whose approach grew from this tradition, it is attentive (though in a deliberative and usually modest way) to the welfare of the population at large and not just the elites. US conservatives like Robert Taft and Robert Dole exemplified this tradition as does Chris Patten of the UK quoted in Chapter 1.

Libertarians are the heirs to nineteenth-century liberalism. They favor individual freedom to the maximum degree possible. This freedom goes beyond free markets to include the social sphere. So, unlike many conservatives in the US today, libertarians are likely to favor choice when it comes to abortion policy as well as a minimum of government interference in the personal lives of citizens in general.

Fiscal conservatives focus on shrinking the size and reach of government. They emphasize keeping taxes to a minimum while balancing budgets and avoiding deficits.

Religious conservatives view traditional religion and morality as keys to a sound society. The highly politicized religious right in contemporary America has been particularly active in opposing bans on school prayer and in opposing social changes such as gay marriage that are seen as countering biblical injunctions.

Social conservatives have a broader take on conservatism than religious conservatives in that they emphasize a wider array of traditional values, with emphasis on family life and the preservation of traditional social customs.

Neo-conservatives started as a group of former liberals whose intense anti-communism and militant foreign policy views have slowly been joined to conventional economic views typical of fiscal conservatives. Where once the goal of neo-conservatives was to drag the Republican Party, kicking and screaming into the twentieth century when it comes to social and economic policy,[22] it is now much more aligned with traditional Republican perspectives on the economy. Neocons, as they are often called, were major initiators and supporters of the American invasion of Iraq.

Paleo-conservatives emphasize the traditions of the American past and the celebration of its values. They tend to be isolationists in foreign policy and strongly opposed to high levels of immigration. Pat Buchanan, the author of *Where the Right Went Wrong: How Neoconservatives Subverted the Reagan Revolution and Hijacked the Bush Presidency*, is typical of this genre.[23]

Compassionate conservatives emphasize volunteerism and the role of the private sector in aiding the unfortunate, but they are willing to use the public sector when necessary to achieve these ends.[24]

These types of conservatism often blend into one another, but there is also a potential, realized quite frequently, for conflict. Elite conservatism has been at it most successful politically when differences among the adherents of the various philosophies and emphases are put aside temporarily so that they are willing to work with one another. This was the case when conservatives were willing to follow the tenets of *fusionism*, developed by Frank Meyer of *National Review*, and based on the notion prominent and appealing in the election campaigns of Ronald Reagan, that conservatives need to come together, united by their opposition to communism, to elect one of their own. However, as I said in the article from which this section of the chapter is derived:

> [T]here is constant tension among conservatives at the elite level over principle and practice . . . [T]he type of cautious, undogmatic, and highly practical types who the [Edmund] Burkes and [Chris] Pattens of the world might think of as genuine conservatives have been joined by an often raucous group of highly committed people who identify as conservatives but differ from Burkeans in their stronger commitment to doctrine and their willingness, indeed often eagerness, to make radical changes in government and society.[25]

While the adherents of these various strains of conservatism struggle over doctrine and policy, they do tend to come together in election campaigns because the Democrats usually put up a candidate for partisan office who is more objectionable to them than any opponent within the conservative movement. But the levels of enthusiasm vary, probably confusing many conservatives in the general public who may find some of the points of debate hard to follow.[26]

Endnotes

1 The quotations are from Richard Hayton, *Reconstructing Conservatism? The Conservative Party in Opposition, 1997–2010* (Manchester: Manchester University Press, 2012), pages 6 and 7.

2 Nigel F. B. Allington and Gillian Peele, "The British Conservative Party and Economic Policy," Chapter 6 in Mark McNaught, ed., *Reflections on Conservative Politics in the United Kingdom and the United States* (Lanham, MD: Lexington Books, 2012), page 116.

3 Allington and Peele, "The British Conservative Party and Economic Policy," page 122. See also, Mark Garnett, "Ideology and the Conservative Party," pages 107–124 in Mark Garnett and Philip Lynch, eds. *The Conservatives in Crisis: The Tories after 1997* (Manchester: Manchester University Press, 2003), especially pages 108–110.

4 "Margaret Thatcher: A Life in Quotes," *The Guardian*, April 8, 2013, http://www.theguardian.com/politics/2013/apr/08/margaret-thatcher-quotes.

5 Quoted in R. W. Apple, Jr., "Macmillan, at 90, Rouses the Lords," *New York Times,* November 14, 1984, http://www.nytimes.com/1984/11/14/world/macmillan-at-90-rouses-the-lords.html.

6 Tim Bale, *The Conservative Party: From Thatcher to Cameron* (Cambridge: Polity Press, 2010), page 1.

7   Bale, *The Conservative Party* (2010), pages 365–373. The quotations are from pages 365 and 373.

8   Bale, *The Conservative Party* (2010). For quoted phrases in the paragraph, see pages 378, 381 and 391.

9   Richard Hayton, *Reconstructing Conservatism?* (2012); the quotations are from pages 146 and 147.

10 For a brief piece on the Big Society, see Vernon Bogdanor, "David Cameron's Legacy Depends on Making Big Society Work," *Independent*, June 24, 2015, http://www.independent.co.uk/voices/comment/david-cameron-s-legacy-depends-on-making-the-big-society-work-10343006.html. For a brief and very critical view, see Simon Griffiths, "Cameron's 'Progressive Conservatism' Is Largely Cosmetic and Without Substance," July 19, 2012, http://blogs.lse.uk.politicsand policy/2012/07/19/.

11 John F. Burns and Alan Cowell, "British House of Commons Approves Gay Marriage," *New York Times*, February 5, 2013, http://www.nytimes.com/2013/02/06/world/europe/britain-gay-marriage-vote.html. A Reuters article in the *New York Times*, stressed the tensions within the Conservative Party over the gay marriage legislation: "Gay Marriage Law Strains UK Cameron's Leadership, Government," http://www.reuters.com/article/us-britain-cameron-idUSBRE94J0LD20130520. And an article in the *Guardian* by Nicholas Watt (February 5, 2013) featured remarks by a gay Conservative during the debate warning members not to follow the road of the US Republicans lest they risk losing the coming election. See Nicholas Watt, "Gay Marriage Debate: Tory Warns Party Not to Follow the Republican Road," http://www.guardian.co.uk/society/2013/feb/05/.

12 For an interesting take on the role of the state in practice under Conservative Party modernization, see Martin Smith, "Conservative Party Modernisation 2: From Big Society to Small State," April 6, 2015, https://www.psa.ac.uk/insight-plus/blog/conservative-party-modernisation-2-big-society-small-state.

13 Richard Hayton, *Reconstructing Conservatism?* (2012), page 98.

14 See Nolan McCarty, Keith T. Poole, and Howard Rosenthal, *Polarized America* (Cambridge: MIT, 2006), page 11. A particularly sharp and straightforward statement about this phenomenon can be found in Christopher Hare, Keith T. Poole and Howard Rosenthal, "Polarization in Congress Has Risen Sharply. Where Is It Going Next?" *Washington Post*. Monkey Cage, February 2012. They note in reference to congressional polarization: "the dramatic shift to the right by the Republican Party."

15 Matt Grossman and David A. Hopkins, "Ideological Republicans and Group Interest Democrats: The Asymmetry of American Party Politics," *Perspectives on Politics*, Vol. 13, No. 1 (March 2015), page 119.

16 Thomas E. Mann and Norman J. Ornstein, *It's Even Worse Than It Looks: How the American Constitutional System Collided with the New Politics of Extremism* (New York: Basic Books, 2012) and "Let's Just Say It: The Republicans Are The Problem," *Washington Post*, April 27, 2012.

17 See "New Research Shows Ethnic Minority Votes Up for Grabs," *British Future*, May 25, 2015, http://www.britishfuture.org/articles/.

18 Gillian Peele, "Religion and Conservatism in the United Kingdom," Chapter 4 in Mark McNaught, ed., *Reflections on Conservative Politics in the United Kingdom and the United States*, pages 81–98, especially page 81.

19 Tim Bale, *The Conservative Party* (2010) page 11.

20 See Tim Bale and Paul Webb, "Not as Bad as We Feared or Even Worse Than We Imagined? Assessing and Explaining Conservative Party Members' Views on Coalition," *Political Studies*, Vol. 64(1) (2014), pages 1–20.

21 This part of the chapter is an expanded version of the "What Is Conservatism?" section of "Understanding American Political Conservatism," in Robert Scott and Stephan Kosslyn, eds., *Emerging Trends in the Social and Behavioral Sciences,* John Wiley and Sons, 2015.

22 Irving Kristol stated the goal of neoconservatism as follows: "to convert the Republican Party, and American conservatism in general, against their respective wills, into a new kind of politics suitable to governing a modern democracy. See Irving Kristol, "The Neoconservative Persuasion," *Weekly Standard,* August 25, 2003.

23 Patrick J. Buchanan, *Where the Right Went Wrong: How Neoconservatives Subverted the Reagan Revolution and Hijacked the Bush Presidency* (New York: Thomas Dunne Books, 2004).

24 For an excellent essay on compassionate conservatism, see Steven Teles, "Compassionate Conservatism, Domestic Policy, and the Politics of Ideational Change," Chapter 9, pages 178–211 in Joel D. Aberbach and Gillian Peele, *Crisis of Conservatism: The Republican Party, the Conservative Movement and American Politics after Bush* (New York: Oxford University Press, 2011).

25 Joel D. Aberbach, *Understanding American Political Conservatism* (2015), page 3.

26 Indeed, an important area for future research is to determine how much, if at all, the more subtle aspects of conservative doctrine and doctrinal debate impact the public.

9 Contemporary American Conservatism
Synopsis, Problems, and Prospects

There was trouble in the US in 1965, but also great optimism about the possibility of a more harmonious future. As historian James T. Patterson records in his preface to *The Eve of Destruction: How 1965 Transformed America*: "Many contemporary observers [were] caught up in the triumphalism of the time," with the defeat of conservative Republican Barry Goldwater in the 1964 presidential election and the imminent passage of Lyndon Johnson's Great Society Programs. He quotes James MacGregor Burns' view that "this is as surely the liberal epoch as the late 19th century was a conservative one," and cites the title of a story in *Time* magazine that characterized the US as "On the Fringe of a Golden Era." Indeed, Patterson notes that "Many political commentators were so awed by these [the 1964 election] results that they wondered if conservatism – or even the two-party system – would survive."[1]

A leading political scientist published an article on "The Politics of Consensus in an Age of Affluence" that concluded:

> The headlines will not show this consensus, nor will the demonstrations at city hall or on the campus, but the ordinary man in the Age of Affluence is beginning to find some greater sense of hope and peace and self-assurance expressed in a less acrimonious political style.[2]

However, American society and politics went through changes in the following years that witnessed not rising consensus but conflict that increased in many areas and hardened in others. Rather than a working class that Robert E. Lane conjectured would remain strongly Democratic and a middle class that would tend increasingly towards a liberal Republican bent, or a rising tide of industrialists and businessmen who would see that the liberal policies of the welfare state provide "the basis for the prosperity and growth in which they share," the country experienced a reordering of the polity that hardened lines and made it more conflictual. Lane's essay speculated (correctly, as it turned out) that "the Republican party, having lost almost all of its Negro following, may come to believe that it is in its interest to stress 'states rights,' 'law and order in the streets,' and 'voluntarism in school assignments,' and other themes with barely disguised racial appeal," leading to situations where "racial voting, unlike class voting, will take on a new intensity and move away from the politics of consensus." But he was optimistic that this would not happen, at least for most of the population, because racial issues in the end would not trump other factors in partisan choice.[3]

We now know that the latter was too optimistic a view, but in all candor it was the view I shared after the 1964 election, and not just because I was one of Professor Lane's students and many admirers. Vietnam was not yet the complete tragedy it turned out to be for the US and, on the domestic front, there was a list of enacted changes that promised a plethora of improvements in life for all. Blacks would finally be able to register and vote in large numbers, bringing to fruition one of the major goals of the civil rights movement and ending the sad tale of disenfranchisement in the South. Medicare would provide decent health care for the elderly. Poverty would be at least lessened. Technology would provide greater productivity and improved decision making and, with it, a more harmonious and consensual society. The conservatives of the nation would be like the "One Nation" conservatives of the UK, cautious and thoughtful consolidators of progress. The liberals would be pushing for continued change, but mindful of the need to work with those on the other side as US politics returned to a more normal, i.e. pre-1964 landslide, situation where the support of at least part of the opposition was necessary to achieve major legislative ends.

But this kind of consensus-oriented politics was not what the future had in store. A disastrous war would rip society apart. Changes brought about by the civil rights movement, changes long needed in the US, would unsettle many and would impact politics and partisanship, particularly in the South, in a huge way. Values would change rapidly, especially among those who were in the vanguard of change, and then spread to many others who were less involved, with a backlash from many traditionalists. The economy would be buffeted by deindustrialization and a coincident decline of organized labor and the role it played in politics. In short, the conditions that would ordinarily be expected to underlay consensus gave way to conditions more conducive to division, despite the continued affluence of a good part of the citizenry.

This book focuses on two aspects of politics in the years since the 1960s – the conservatism of much of the US population and the changing dynamics of political conservatism, especially among the general public, but with some attention to elite divisions as well. The cause of conservatism Goldwater set out to champion, declared Theodore White in his book on the debacle that was the 1964 election, had been "exposed as formless in ideas and hollow in program."[4] Certainly, it looked that way in the defeat of conservatism's then major political figure. But that cause, and certainly the attraction of the conservative label, did not simply go away as a result of the political landslide that buried the Republican Party in 1964. If anything, identification with conservatism gained strength in the disillusioning years that followed and continued as a major force, and the political and institutional forces supporting conservatism grew in size, number, and influence.[5]

The core of the book is an examination of the prominent level of self-identified conservatism in the US public in the years since the 1960s and especially of the nature of changes in the correlates of conservatism that mark an evolving set of linkages making mass conservatism a potent political force. That analysis is supplemented by a comparative examination of elite data suggesting that ideological division (polarization as some prefer to term it) is not just an elite phenomenon, especially for those in the public with high levels of education. Further, after a comparison of conservative party politics in the United Kingdom and the United States in the contemporary period, especially of the changes that the UK conservatives have made to increase their electoral appeal, I argue that the nature of conservative strength in the US and the impact of that strength on the chances for continued victory in elections to at least some of the electoral bodies of the government diminishes the incentives for conservative US politicians to modify their positions significantly or for conservative identifiers in the public, especially those who identify strongly as conservatives, to see the reasons for them to do so.

To recapitulate briefly, available evidence suggests that the United States went from a nation with relatively equal percentages of the population who identified as conservatives or liberals, that is, where there was a balance between the two, to one where conservatives became the modal group and have continued to be so. While it is only an inference, the change from balance to a more prominent place for conservative identification appears to have happened during the period of change and turmoil in the 1960s, especially in the time after the 1964 election, the passage of Great Society legislation that followed, and the dramatic escalation of the Vietnam War and domestic unrest that was coincident with it. Certainly, by 1976 more people identified as some type of conservative than as either a moderate or some type of liberal, and that pattern is consistent in the years thereafter.

Though the level of conservatism has remained more or less constant, its political correlates have evolved significantly. One basic change in the years covered by the data analyzed in the book is seen in the South, where the relationship between party identification and conservative identification has been transformed over time, going from a mild relationship between the two (making the South distinctive in this regard), to a high level (making the South typical of the rest of the country in this respect at least, and solidly Republican). This is an element of a growing confluence between party, conservatism and vote choice as part of a nationally converging, ideologically identified political culture.[6] Where in the not too distant past the South provided an anomalous group of politicians elected to the House and Senate who were, in terms of their politics, by and large Democrats in name only (DINOS, some might say today), now these same Members of Congress and Senators are mainly Republicans (often by switching parties in earlier years), at least those who do not represent districts with African American majorities, and the important role in bargaining and deal-making that many Southern Democrats had, both through their seniority and their positions as conservative-leaning politicians in a liberal-leaning party, is now replaced by even greater rigidity and division.[7]

Another change is in the relationship between views on abortion and ideology. Where once the relationship was relatively weak, it is now quite strong. And the same holds true of religiosity and to a lesser extent of views on whether or not the government should provide a guarantee of people's jobs and standard of living. (The relationship was strong and relatively the same over time with views on government assistance to African Americans.) A key factor here is that two phenomena are occurring simultaneously with respect to the relationship of ideology to both abortion policy and religiosity; while people report less religious service attendance and greater support for a woman's right to choose, the relationship of views on abortion and of religiosity with ideology has grown stronger over time. In short, these areas are more politicized, with conservatives more differentiated from liberals in the later years than they were in 1972. And that politicization is occurring at the same time that the public overall is, if anything, once again moving in a slightly more liberal direction on abortion[8] and indicators of religiosity in the population at large are showing a decline. The net result is greater division between conservatives and liberals and consequently a greater significance to the continued conservatism that marks much of the public in that there is increasing differentiation between conservatives and liberals in these areas. All this is reflected in the increase in explanatory power of the simple model used in Chapter 5 to predict conservatism and the closing circle of ideology described in the previous paragraph and in Chapter 5.

Beyond the over-time comparisons, there are a rich array of findings on values, cultural views and views on race that help to delineate what it now tends to mean to identify as a conservative.[9] Of particular importance here are the strong relationships between conservatism and traditional perspectives on social and religious life as well as the continuing import of that seemingly eternal divider in the United States – race. The latter is no longer reflected in views on segregation – at least it is hard to find this out because the term is no longer in widespread use and therefore not directly measured in surveys like the ANES – but by other sorts of takes on race. For example, the more conservative one is the more likely one is to feel that we have gone too far in pushing equal rights in this country, or to believe that the Obama administration favors blacks over whites, or to oppose affirmative action in universities or in the workplace (a widely shared view that is even more prominent among conservatives than among others), and, in what was probably the ultimate test of such views during the Obama years, to doubt that the President was born in the United States. On the values and culture front, to take some examples, the more conservative one says one is, the more likely he or she is to favor the use of the death penalty for those convicted of murder, to oppose gay marriage and to show little tolerance for newer lifestyles. And the more conservative one is the more likely an individual is to believe that controlling illegal immigration is an important goal for US policy. In short, and in line with the general view, US conservatives are traditionalists and, while they may change their views on social and cultural issues over time, they are clearly slower than others to do so.

An illustration of both traditionalism and change can be seen on a topic that roiled American politics for many years – whether or not gays should be allowed to serve openly in the military. Table 9.1 tells a fascinating story. In 1992, a majority of respondents in the ANES survey favored allowing gays to serve in the military, though the percentage was less than 60 percent (58.4). Over the next 20 years that percentage rose

Table 9.1 Percent Saying Gays Should Be Allowed to Serve in the Military, by Ideology, 1992–2012*

Year	Gamma	% Among "Extremely Conservative" Respondents	% Among All Conservative Respondents	% Among All Respondents
1992	.41	27.6	43.0	58.3
1996	.40	31.3	56.6	68.7
2000	.37	36.5	65.9	79.1
2004	.35	34.1	75.0	81.1
2008	.32	59.6	73.0	79.8
2012	.43	56.9	76.6	85.1

Data Source: 1992–2012 ANES

Note: African American respondents filtered out.

*Percentages = FEEL STRONGLY plus FEEL NOT STRONGLY. See question wording below.

Question wording:

Ideology measure: Where would you place YOURSELF on this scale, or haven't you thought much about this? Extremely Liberal; Liberal; Slightly Liberal; Moderate; Middle of the Road; Slightly Conservative; Conservative; Extremely Conservative.

Homosexuals in the military: Do you think homosexuals should be allowed to serve in the United States Armed Forces or don't you think so?

Do you feel STRONGLY or NOT STRONGLY that homosexuals should/should not be allowed to serve?

to 85.1. A consistent relationship between conservatism and ideology was in evidence throughout the period. What in essence happened was that conservatives moved with the rest of the country to greater acceptance of the idea of gays serving in the military, but they were always a step behind liberals and moderates in this regard. And the degree of their conservatism determined how much behind others they were in accepting this change.[10]

In short, conservatives continued to be more opposed to this change than others over the years, but they were also clearly impacted by at least some broader cultural trends. This can be seen as an example of what conservatism is when playing its traditional role – more resistant to change than others, but accepting change as the broader society adapts over time, in this case to acceptance of the rights of a group whose legitimacy was questioned by many in the past. I'll return to this in the last part of the chapter (and cover the topic from a different perspective in Chapter 8), but one of the delicate tasks of conservatism and of the political parties that identify with it is to recognize when changes that might previously have been unacceptable to many of their adherents have built to a point where they have become "mainstream," and where pragmatism, as well as in this case a recognition of the rights of others, calls for an adjustment.

The academic literature addresses another area (beyond changing values in the broader culture) where conservative elites are well advised to tread carefully. This is the notion that while the American public may be "philosophically conservative," it is "operationally liberal" (see Chapter 4). Conservatives and liberals in the general public are clearly split on philosophical positions about the size and role of government. Of that there is little doubt. But when it comes to them operationalizing these beliefs, the story is often more complex. (Conservatives tend to want spending to stay at current levels – and less often than liberals to want increases in public spending – but they still tend to balk at cuts.) The survey data show some movement in this area in 2012, with slipping overall support, especially among conservatives, for increased federal spending. While this can be seen as a victory of sorts for fiscal conservatives, it is still the case that the public – including much of the conservative part of it – continues to favor the spending funds on the government programs and services it receives.[11]

This important area aside, however – and it is a difficult one for conservative elites to manage, though some try to have it both ways by claiming that they can maintain many services, cut taxes, and increase the revenues to provide funding for popular programs through the "supply side" miracle of substantial economic growth that would supposedly follow a cut in taxes and regulations – the division between conservatives and liberals is strong and consistent enough to make many worry about political polarization and its effects. As Chapter 6 notes, there is a large debate about whether to call the phenomenon we are witnessing polarization or sorting, but there is no doubt that divisions in the Congress have increased and evidence in that chapter indicates that the divisions evident in many of the nation's elites are mirrored in the public, and to an equal extent among the well-educated part of it.

The emergence of the Tea Party in 2009 is a stunning symbol (and reality) of contemporary conservatism. As Chapter 7 shows, there is a huge overlap between Tea Party support and conservative (and Republican) identification, with the most conservative people also the strongest supporters of the Tea Party. In effect, as the analysis suggests, backing for the Tea Party is a manifestation of the commitment and discontent of the most conservative wing of the Republican Party. Supporters are major players in the Republican nominating process because they participate in party primaries or caucuses at higher rates than more moderate types. This gives them (and the most strongly conservative wing of the party of which they are in essence a part) an inordinate influence in the Republican nominating process and on the behavior of Republican candidates. Elected officials, therefore, tend to pay them special heed. Their influence comes from high rates of participation, a sign of their intensity, something politicians respect because of the damage it can do them. As Chapter 7 concludes, "Republican elected officials generally pay a lot of attention to these folks because they have relatively little choice, and those whose candidacies depend on primaries or caucuses (which is most of them) are at minimum torn between what are often the broader views of their constituencies and the views of those who play a disproportionate role in selecting them to run for office."

The extremism of the candidates the Tea Party helps nominate and the positions it pushes elected officials to support often repel more moderate conservative voters and, in that way, may well hurt the Republican Party more than it helps. In any event, the Tea Party – and the sentiments it represents – is certainly a major force inhibiting change in a more moderate direction, the topic of Chapter 8. One irony is that democratic processes in the form of primaries tend to give added influence to the more extreme wings of the parties, be they left or right. In the US, primaries have certainly helped the Tea Party and in the UK, the Labour Party primary process used in 2015 made Jeremy Corbyn, a previously un-influential Member of Parliament on the left of the party, its leader.[12]

To summarize very briefly, the argument is that reactions to the events of the 1960s probably increased the level of professed conservatism in the United States, which has remained the modal position of the public at least since the early 1970s. While the percentage of the non-African American public who identify as conservatives has not changed much since then (hovering around 43 percent), the political significance of that conservatism has changed significantly. Conservatism, party identification and the vote are now tightly entwined throughout the country, resulting in a realignment of Southern politics that has had a huge impact on the Republican Party. Over time, as well, there has been a tightening of the links between conservatism and religiosity, opposition to abortion, and views on the government's role in the economy, that, along with notions about race and numerous social issues now define conservatism in this country. Politically charged court decisions, such as Roe v. Wade in 1973 on abortion rights eventually became, and fear that the nation's family and moral base were being undermined by liberal policies, magnified by fears that the IRS would deny tax exemptions to Christian schools because of de-facto segregation, were pivotal to the formation of the Moral Majority in 1979 and later of the Christian Coalition and have contributed to the shape and increased political clout of conservatism.[13] Indeed, conservatism is now a major force in American politics, and its problems and prospects are a subject that, while they would not have attracted huge attention in the wake of the 1964 election, are now undeniably of great import.

What about the Future?

Problems and Potential Problems

Conservatives and conservatism are strong now, but could face many future problems.

First there is a potential demographic problem. As of now, African Americans are, for the most part, lost to the Republicans who in the contemporary period are the party of conservatism. There is nothing on the horizon that is likely to change that. Moreover, disputes about immigration policy, especially the kind of debates that marked the Republican presidential primary campaigns in 2011–2012 and 2015–2016 and that are manifested in other ways as well, may easily move Latinos into the same partisan position that blacks are in at this time – strong opponents of the Republican Party – even though many of the social positions taken by conservatives might have appeal to Latino voters. Indeed, the general problem flowing from positions candidates claiming to be conservatives take on Mexican and Central American immigration (such as Mitt Romney's infamous statement on "self-deportation") risk spreading a general image that conservatives are unfriendly to immigrants in general, something potentially very costly in a nation with a large immigrant population.

Second, values change, sometimes rapidly, and we know that there are several trends that should worry conservatives. To take one example, conservatives do best among those who are regular attendees at religious services, but we know that number is dropping. The country has been becoming more secular, and that trend is likely to continue if the US follows the path of most West European nations. A second example, discussed earlier in the chapter, is what happened with public opposition to gays in the military (and later with opposition to gay marriage) – it evaporated in a short period of time. Conservatives are still more likely to oppose gays in the military than others, but the issue has gone from being a political asset to one that is uncomfortable for them (libertarians excepted) and could undermine the conservative brand by making its adherents seem out of touch rather than simply the holders of traditional values. Indeed, the danger to the conservative "brand" is that many of conservatism's adherents, especially the most passionate ones, will be seen as increasingly out of touch and intolerant rather than as the bedrock holders of traditional values, an oft-admired conservative virtue.

Third, while race, what years ago Gunnar Myrdal so aptly terms "An American Dilemma," is a general subject of concern in the United States, it presents special problems for conservatives.[14] Our society has made numerous, if fitful and inadequate, advances in race relations, but it obviously still has a long way to go. Republican conservatives have reaped clear short-term advantages from the so-called "Southern strategy" because the views of conservatives fit that strategy well, but over the long term, in a country that is predicted to be "majority minority" by 2044 (and for children, by 2020) that is a very large potential problem for both the Republican Party and conservative politics. Efforts to keep minorities off the voting rolls may work in the short term, but they will just exacerbate dislike of Republicans in the longer run among blacks and other minorities, especially Latinos, and, by extension, of the conservatism identified with Republicans. As the brief description of traditional conservatism in Chapter 1 should suggest, racial bias is not inherent in conservatism, but the views of many conservatives probably make it seem so to many African Americans and others, and that is, in the long term, not in the interest of the Republican Party or, indeed, the nation.

A fourth possible problem is in the area of federal government spending. The "philosophical conservative, operational liberal" phenomenon discussed earlier in the chapter is not much of a problem as long as spending for popular programs is basically maintained. Calls for controlling spending by conservative activists and elites have relatively little effect on benefits in that circumstance. But actual success in cutting popular programs might be another matter. As of now, there is little chance of that, but, ironically, if the most conservative elements in Congress should succeed in making significant cuts, that could have negative effects on many voters who identify as conservatives.

A fifth problem flows out of the widespread use of primaries to select candidates for office. Given the tendency of the most strongly identified conservatives to participate more than others (and almost exclusively now, with the South a Republican region, in the Republican primaries) as well as the impact of highly motivated conservative funders and organizations, there is a tendency for relatively extreme candidates to win primaries and, in some cases, to lose the subsequent election. When they do win primaries and succeed in the general election they become part of the face of conservatism and of the Republican Party. The risk here, as I just said, is that these elected officials come to define conservatism.

Sixth, there are numerous conservative factions within the political elite groups. This is part of the vitality of conservatism, but it produces intense infighting at times that has the potential to divide adherents, as the fall of Speaker of the House John Boehner in 2015 demonstrates.[15]

Finally, in a subject discussed at some length in Chapter 8 and in the introduction to this chapter, the strength of conservatives in Congress – a function of the nominating system, of the concentration of Democratic votes in the urban areas, and, since 2010, of redistricting following the big Republican win in the elections of that year – gives conservatives relatively little incentive to make adjustments when things are not going well. They just about always stand a reasonably good chance of winning, or winning back, the presidency or controlling at least one house of Congress and, therefore, are not likely to experience the string of defeats that might encourage change. Aside from a possible image problem with the moderate segment of the general public that can come from the resultant inflexibility, it also goes against the evolutionary grain of traditional conservatism and risks making American conservatism more of a reactionary than a conservative orientation.

Advantages

I've gone through a catalogue of problems, one that is probably incomplete. But what are the advantages? I should say at the outset that, as much of the data analyzed in the book show, they are considerable.

First is the obvious: When asked to identify themselves along the conservative/liberal spectrum, conservative has been the modal choice for most of the period covered by this study (slightly over 40 percent, on average since 1972). That percentage has not varied much, and we know that the measurement is highly reliable because people give basically the same answer to the question when it is asked months apart. It is one of the reasons that Republican politicians, representing what is now the party of choice among conservatives, want to identify themselves as conservatives and, often, as more conservative than their opponents, especially in primary elections.

Second, the conservative movement is served by a large number of think tanks and publications that give it vitality, providing employment for conservative intellectuals and policy ideas and backup for conservative leaders.

Third, there is a great deal of money, both from foundations and individual donors, which support conservatism through contributions to organizations and political campaigns. And, there are now several overtly conservative universities providing additional support for the training of future leaders.[16]

Fourth, aside from its general strength, there is a tendency of the public to turn to conservatives in time of peril, especially during domestic or foreign disorder. They represent strength in the literal sense and often are the most vociferous patriots.

Finally, there is little doubt that conservative media play a big role, both in defining conservatism and in legitimating the positions of conservative politicians and intellectuals. The ANES data, for example, indicate that many conservatives in the general public are viewers of Fox News and, as mentioned above, there is also a lively network of conservative periodicals and products from conservative think tanks. As an example, in 2012 over 42 percent (42.9) of the "Extremely Conservative" respondents to the ANES survey reported that they regularly watched Bill O'Reilly (the most popular of the Fox News shows) on Fox and over 34 percent (34.4) of respondents who simply chose the "Conservative" option reported the same. (Only 2 percent of liberals gave this answer.)[17] The figures for conservatives may exaggerate the viewership, but they are stunning nonetheless. There is tremendous penetration of conservative media into the conservative segment of the public.

A Final Comment

As I write the conclusion to this book in early 2016, conservatism is, in the language of advertising, a strong brand in the United States. It is popular with a large segment of the public. Its adherents at the elite level are active, well-funded, and quite successful in elections. They have a strong base as a result of increasing success in elections in the South as well as in other areas around the country. Conservatives are hugely influential in the House of Representatives and, to a somewhat lesser extent, in the Senate as well. The changes that have taken place over the last half century have contributed to a conservatism that overall is well grounded in the views of its adherents in the general public as well as among segments of the elite. But there are weaknesses as well, and demographic changes and changing public values in addition to possible intense infighting among conservative factions could undermine the current conservative strengths. One thing is almost certain: Edmund Burke, and those whose conservatism follows in the path he set, would be hard-pressed to recognize much of what we now call conservatism in the US.

Endnotes

1 James T. Patterson, *The Eve of Destruction: How 1965 Transformed America* (New York: Basic Books, 2012). The quoted material is from pages xii, and 26, and 253.

2 Robert E. Lane, "The Politics of Consensus in an Age of Affluence," *The American Political Science Review,* Vol. 59, No. 4 (Dec. 1965), page 895.

3 The quotations in this paragraph are from Robert E. Lane, "The Politics of Consensus in an Age of Affluence," pages 880, and 892–893.

4 Theodore H. White, in *The Making of the President 1964* (New York: Harper Perennial 2010 edition of the book originally published in 1965), page 332.

5 For example, see Thomas Medvetz, *Think Tanks in America* (Chicago: University of Chicago Press, 2012), especially pages 238–239 Table B.4 on media citations by think tanks and pages 124–129 on "Think Tanks and the Rise of the Right," and Donald E. Abelson, *Do Think Tanks Matter? Assessing the Impact of Public Policy Institutes,* Second Edition (Montreal & Kingston: McGill-Queen's University Press, 2009), especially pages 96 and 202 on newspaper citations and references in the US Congress. For an excellent account of conservative influence in legal reform, see Steven M. Teles, *The Rise of the Conservative Legal Movement: The Battle for Control of the Law* (Princeton: Princeton University Press, 2008).

6 I don't mean by this that all regions are the same in terms of partisan support, but that the dynamics of politics in terms of the relationship between party, ideology and vote are now the same.

7 Ira Katznelson and Quinn Malloy, "Was the South Pivotal? Situated Partisanship and Policy Coalitions during the New Deal and Fair Deal," *The Journal of Politics,* Vol. 74, No. 2 (April 2012), page 617, write about the Southern members of the House and Senate during the New Deal and Fair Deal period stressing what they call "'situated partisanship,' an approach that privileges temporality and policy substance to understand when and with regard to which issues political parties are able to organize the preferences of their members and control lawmaking" (page 604). By the end of the period covered (1952), Southern Democrats were splitting more and more with their party (page 616), as southerners "were put under stress by how [they] reconciled their preference for racial hierarchy with the advantages of party cohesion" (page 618).

8 See Lydia Saad, "Americans Chose 'Pro-Choice' for the First Time in Seven Years," Gallup Social Issues, May 29, 2005, http://www.gallup.com/poll/183434/americans-choose-pro-choice-first-time-seven-years.aspx.

9 Please note, of course, that not every conservative would hold precisely the same views in these areas. It would be useful in future research to focus on analysis of the relationship of the indicators to one another and to scale many of the items used.

10 Even among "Extremely Conservative" respondents, the percentage accepting the change rose from 27.6 to 56.9 over the 20-year period.

11 Keep in mind that cutting spending, especially on programs for the disadvantaged, is a big issue in US conservative politics, but not necessarily a tenet of conservatism.

12 For some early information on and analysis of the Corbyn victory, see Rowena Mason, "Labour Leadership: Jeremy Corbyn Elected with Huge Mandate," *The Guardian,* September 12, 2015, http://theguardian.com/politics/2015/sep/12; Steven Erlanger, "Labour Party's Swerve Left May Help Tories in Next British Elections," *New York Times,* September 13, 2015, http://www.nytimes.com/; and Patrick Wintour, "The Jeremy Corbyn Victory Scenario: Confrontation or Cooperation," *The Guardian,* August 31, 2015, http:///www.theguardian.com/politics/2015/aug/31.

13 William Martin, *With God on Our Side: The Rise of the Religious Right in America* (New York: Broadway Books, 2005), especially pages 173 and 194.

14 Mrydal's book is: Gunnar Myrdal, *An American Dilemma: The Negro Problem and American Democracy* (New York: Harper, 1944).
15 See Jennifer Steinhauer, "John Boehner, House Speaker Will Resign from Congress," *New York Times*, September 25, 2015; and Carl Hulse, "Paul Ryan Lands at the Center of a Rivalry for the Soul of the GOP," *New York Times*, November 2, 2015. Both can be found at: http://www.nytimes.com/.
16 For example, see the list of top conservative colleges now on the Young America's Foundation web site (www.yaf.org). These include Liberty University, Hillsdale College and Regent University.
17 The correlation (gamma) of the ideology measure and viewing of O'Reilly on Fox is a stunning .67.

Afterword

May 27, 2016

The main text of this book was completed at the beginning of January 2016. The predominant view at that time was that Donald Trump's effort to secure the Republican nomination would fail. This afterword is being written in May 2016 and at this point Trump is the "presumptive nominee" of the Republican Party. His successful campaign for the nomination has set off a vigorous debate focusing on the man himself, his past history and his values, as well as his likely prospects in the November election. But for our purposes, other aspects of the discussion are key: How did this happen, and what does Trump's success so far say about the present and future state of American conservatism?

The book emphasizes the large number of Americans who identify as conservatives, and also what people mean when they say they are conservative – who the conservatives are and what they believe. It focuses on the general public over a forty-year period (1972 to 2012), but also considers the views of elites, especially political elites. The findings demonstrate an increasing link within the public between professed conservatism and Republican identification and an increasing link between a variety of social and political beliefs and conservative identification, in other words, an evolving political ideology in the public that showed signs of increasing strength and import over time.

Chapter 9, the concluding chapter, summarizes a set of problems and potential problems that might affect US conservatism in the future as well as the considerable advantages that conservatives and the conservative movement possess. The weaknesses center around a growing problem that stems from the rapidly changing demographic profile of the US, changes in values that are accompanying the rapid economic and technological changes that mark the contemporary United States, tensions between the libertarian-oriented economic philosophy that many US conservatives, especially in the economic and intellectual elite, fully embrace and the views of conservative adherents in the broader population, and the fact that there are many factions within the conservative elite groups with strongly held views, a factor that leads to intense infighting at times. An additional factor identified in the discussion of problems and potential problems is the widespread use of primaries and the fact that those who turn out in primaries may benefit extreme candidates because their supporters often turn out at higher rates than those with more moderate views. Finally, the chapter summarizes the lack of flexibility and, indeed, outright resistance to compromise and change that the US separation of powers system encourages among many congressional conservatives.

The latter point was placed in the context of a comparative analysis of US and UK conservatism, but subsequent events suggest that it did not sufficiently stress the frustration that could result among conservatives themselves and the possibility that this frustration could have a strong and immediate impact on conservative politics. Indeed, several observers stress the frustration many conservatives apparently feel as a result of the failure of conservative politicians to deliver on their promises. This kind of frustration is relative, of course, since those on the other side are also frustrated, but the key point from this perspective is a failure of conservatives to deliver, at least from the point of view of conservative adherents.

Those making this argument point to the conscious policy of the Republican majorities in the House and Senate to reject most of President Obama's initiatives and to undermine those it could not reject as an unintended precursor to the success of Trump. That strategy may have yielded additional conservative strength in the Congress, but, in the words of Norman Ornstein of the American Enterprise Institute, "It's led to all this anger. They tried to make the entire process look ugly and illegitimate. It worked. In the process of winning these short-term victories in the midterms [Ornstein is referring here to the 2010 congressional elections], they laid the groundwork for Trump."[1] John Cassidy, writing in *The New Yorker*, expressed similar sentiments:

> If Republican voters hadn't been so disillusioned by their usual leaders, Trump would have remained a fringe candidate. . . . Instead, aided by some prominent right-wing media figures, . . . the New York businessman was able to present himself as the heir to the Tea Party revolution, which many activists felt had been quashed or betrayed.[2]

In this interpretation of the rise of Trump, Republicans in Congress, while cheered on by many leaders and media figures of the conservative movement as they denounced Obama and at times obstructed the operation of the government, eventually came across as ineffective or worse. That opened the way to the candidacy of someone who could separate himself from the day-to-day strife of ordinary politics and, as Trump's campaign slogan states, promise (by this hypothesis more credibly than a standard politician) to "Make America Great Again."

However, it likely took more than an opening to make the Trump nomination campaign successful. There were factors in the nominating process and in his past experience that aided Trump. One was the number of candidates seeking the nomination. There were 17 to start. This gave someone with the presence and television experience of Donald Trump an opportunity to stand out. It also reduced the probability that any of the candidates would be so strong to start with that he or she would win anything resembling an outright victory in the early primaries. In addition, it meant that as Trump's standing in the polls rose to a level indicating support by a third or more of the Republican primary electorate he would look increasingly like the party's choice even if he did not achieve a majority of those voting. Further, in terms of his style and personality, Trump was able to seize the attention of the media with his tweets and labeling of his opponents and thus gain a huge amount of free publicity. This contributed to the large turnout in the primaries and caucuses, turnout that may well have benefitted Trump more than other candidates.[3]

Finally, as an examination of data from exit polls suggests, Trump's unorthodox package of positions probably helped give him the relatively high level of support he developed across the spectrum of conservative primary voters. One of the things that most impressed me in looking at CNN exit poll data from primaries held in the same 12 states examined in the discussion of turnout above is that while Senator Ted Cruz, the most fixedly conservative in his issue positions of the candidates who eventually stood between Trump and the nomination, showed relatively strong support from Republican voters who identified as "very conservative" and then saw his support drop off across the balance of the ideological spectrum, Trump found support across the board. The two candidates were actually quite close in the average percent of the "very conservative" vote that they got (an average of 39.5 percent of "very conservative respondents reported voting for Trump as opposed to 41.0 percent for Cruz), but Trump averaged about double the percentage of votes he got from the "somewhat conservative" (45.1 percent versus 23.8 percent for Cruz) and he got more than double the percentage of moderates (41.3 percent versus 15.7).[4] In short, while Trump crushed Cruz in the percent of the vote he got from those who identified as "somewhat conservative" or "moderate," he did almost as well as Cruz did among the "very conservative."

That raises the question of how different he was on the issues. And it also raises the related question about the nature of his conservatism, at least as the Republican primary voters seemed to perceive it in terms of their own preferences.

First, on the issues, Trump was in many areas not all that different from the other Republican candidates, although several of his positions shifted over the years to make this the case on some key questions. For example, on abortion, he changed his views to pro-life in 2011 and compared his evolution on the issue to that of Ronald Reagan. In addition, while defending much of the health work done by Planned Parenthood, he came to the position that it should be defunded. Like most conservatives, he favors eliminating Obamacare and replacing it with Health Savings Accounts. And he announced himself a strong supporter of 2nd Amendment (gun) rights as well as eventually issuing a list of Supreme Court picks that was designed to satisfy the conservative constituency.[5]

On the other hand, he took some positions that clearly set him off from his competitors. Most famously, he promised to build a wall along the US border with Mexico and get the Mexicans to pay for it, a position scoffed at by his opponents but apparently well received by Republican voters.[6] And he proposed a temporary ban on Muslims entering the US, again a proposal that conservatives with a strong constitutional orientation might oppose, but likely well received by frightened voters. In addition, while saying that marriage is between a man and a woman, he has been "far more accepting of sexual minorities than his party's leaders have been."[7] In domestic affairs, he opposed changes that cut Social Security and Medicare and in foreign affairs, among other things, he challenged trade agreements that he said were benefitting other nations at the expense of US workers and the US economy.[8]

Opponents early on questioned his conservative bona fides; indeed they went further than that. For example, *National Review*, in an editorial in January of 2016 said the following:

> Trump is a philosophically unmoored political opportunist who would trash the broad conservative ideological consensus within the GOP in favor of a free-floating populism with strong-man overtones.

The editorial went on to criticize his personal style, especially what it characterized as his "obsession" with winning no matter what the means which it regarded as "anathema to the ordered liberty that conservatives hold dear."[9]

This debate about whether or not Trump is a true conservative continues, although it has receded somewhat now (May 2016) that Trump is acknowledged as the party's nominee. For example, an article in the *New York Times* headlined "Social Conservatives, However Reluctant, Are Warming to the Idea of Trump," emphasized that groups such as Concerned Women of America are moving towards Trump because members fear Hillary Clinton more and have been heartened by Trump's suggestion that he would appoint justices to the Supreme Court who would reverse Roe v. Wade.[10]

Conclusion

Clearly, Trump has shaken up Republican and conservative politics and, certainly if he wins the 2016 election, American politics as well. Students of politics will have many areas to examine. What were the key attitudes that led those who might ordinarily have followed the lead of establishment conservative figures to vote for Donald Trump, especially in the primaries? More generally, what about so-called "populistic conservatism" appealed to voters? We know that conservatives, especially those who identify as "extremely conservative," often hold views that coincide with hostility to minorities or out-groups. Did views on Mexicans (recall the wall promise) or blacks (recall the data on racial resentments and on the likely birthplace of President Obama in Chapters 3, 5, and 7) override other cues about voting and benefit Trump? Indeed, what was the impact of nativism on voting behavior? Many have speculated about the role of de-industrialization on the success of Trump's efforts to gain the Republican nomination.[11] Lost industrial jobs and opposition to trade agreements were issues in the nominating phase of the 2016 election, and I assume that will continue into the general election campaign. What impact have concerns connected to jobs and trade had on vote choice, especially for those who might have been expected to oppose intervention in the economy by the government? What role did modern popular culture and technology play in boosting Trump to the top of the Republican ticket? Did the brilliant primary campaign Trump ran, one that used free media effectively and apparently benefited from his standing and style as a reality TV performer, overcome whatever ideological faults he may have had from the standpoint of voters? In short, here we have a candidate whose prospects were regarded as dim at best at the beginning of the nominating campaign yet has succeeded beyond expectations. Is this an aberration or a harbinger of things to come that calls for a re-evaluation of what it means to be a conservative, especially what it means for the public at large?

Endnotes

1 Quoted in Lisa Mascaro, "The Honeymoon May Be Over for House Speaker Paul Ryan," *Los Angeles Times,* March 31, 2016, http://www.latimes.com/nation/la-na-paul-ryan-challenge-20160331-story.html.

2 John Cassidy, "How Donald Trump Won the G.O.P. Nomination, *The New Yorker,* may 4, 2016, http://www.newyorker.com/news/john-cassidy/how-donald-trump-won-the-g-o-p-nomination. A stronger version of this argument can be found in Paul Krugman, "Wrath of the Conned," *New York Times*, April 29, 2016, http://www.nytimes.com/2016/04/29/opinion/wrath-of-the-conned.html.

3 I took a sample consisting of 12 states holding primaries between February 9 and May 3 in 2016. Republican primary turnout in these states was up 77.9 percent over 2012. The states are: Alabama, Florida, Indiana, Illinois, Michigan, Missouri, New Hampshire, New York, Pennsylvania, Texas, Virginia, and Wisconsin. The source is: Michael P. McDonald, "United States Election Project," http://www.electproject.org/.

4 The states were the same as those listed in note 3 above. The source is: http://www.cnn.com/election/primaries/polls.

5 See "On the Issues," http://www.ontheissues.org/Donald_Trump.htm, for information on Trump's positions over time on a variety of major issues. On the Supreme Court list, see Alan Rappeport and Charlie Savage, "Donald Trump Releases List of Supreme Court Picks," *New York Times*, May 18, 2016, http://www.nytimes.com/2016/05/19/us/politics/donald-trump-supreme-court-nominees.htmlhttp://www.nytimes.com/2016/05/19/us/politics/donald-trump-supreme-court-nominees.html.

6 For Trump's written position on the wall, see his campaign web site: https://www.donaldjtrump.com/positions/immigration-reform.

7 Maggie Haberman, "Donald Trump's More Accepting Views on Gay Issues Set Him Apart in G.O.P., *New York Times,* April 22, 2016, http://www.nytimes.com/2016/04/23/us/politics/donald-trump-gay-rights.html.

8 See http://www.ontheissues.org/Donald_Trump.htm.

9 The quotations in this paragraph are from The Editors, "Against Trump," *National Review*, January 21, 2016, http://www.nationalreview.com/article/430137/donald-trump-conservative-movement-menace

10 See Jeremy Peters, "Social Conservatives, However Reluctant, Are Warming to the Idea of Trump, *New York Times,* May 15, 2016, http://www.nytimes.com/2016/05/16/us/politics/donald-trump-conservatives.html. For an article on the emerging embrace of Trump by many party figures, see Alan Rappeport, "G.O.P. Is Coming Around in Its Embrace of Donald Trump," May 13, 2016, http://www.nytimes.com/2016/05/14/us/politics/gop-is-coming-around-in-its-embrace-of-donald-trump.html.

11 See, for example, Thomas B. Edsall, "Why Trump Now?" *New York Times,* March 1, 2016, http://www.nytimes.com/2016/03/02/opinion/campaign-stops/why-trump-now.html.

Index